Seafarers!

Seafarers!

A strategic missionary vision

Martin Otto

piquant

First edition 2002
08 07 06 05 04 03 02 7 6 5 4 3 2 1

ISBN 0-9535757-6-4

Published by Piquant
PO Box 83, Carlisle, CA3 9GR, United Kingdom
E-mail: info@piquant.net
Website: www.piquant.net
Also published in German: *Seeleute – ein vergessesenes Volk?*
(Hamburg: Verlag C.M.Fliss, 2001) ISBN 3-931188-48-5

Photographs: Martin Otto
Cover design: Paul Lewis

Contents

List of Photographs

All the colour photographs, which have been reproduced in black-and-white in this book, are copyright by Martin Otto.

Foreword

God is a God of seafarers! I have learned that lesson in a very practical way through my brother-in-law, Martin Otto. At the beginning of the 1980s, when he enthusiastically talked about the large ships anchored in the port of Hamburg, he also mentioned the untried possibilities for evangelization. There are so many seafarers from all corners of the globe who do not know the message of the gospel, yet they are open to thinking about what it means and are willing to respond to it. At that time, hundreds of Bible school students in the eastern part of Switzerland were preparing for missionary service at home and abroad. Martin reasoned that a diversity of countries were also represented at the port of Hamburg, and therefore missionary work could be carried out there. I needed proof of this. Sceptical, but nevertheless motivated, I accompanied him on some of his visits to the ships.

My observations matched his descriptions. As a missiologist, one of my projects at that time was to study a particular Muslim ethnic group that intentionally isolated itself from Christianity. I asked myself the question, how could they hear about Christ when the missionary efforts in their country were continually thwarted by their government. In 1996, when a part of the Gospels was finally made available in their language, the team of Seamen's Christian Friend Society was able to distribute it in Hamburg and other ports. Although the Islamic government publicly prohibited the possession of such literature, seafarers were extremely interested in it.

Many challenges and questions had to be dealt with in the founding years of this missionary work. How can seafarers who have accepted Christ into their lives be followed up and given support? How can seafarers grow spiritually in their environment? Will seafarers have a spiritual home when, after months at sea, they are on land again for a period of time? Is there a legitimate form of church which does not meet on land but at sea instead?

By means of a carefully thought-out Bible correspondence programme as well as a communications system for sharing information between the ports worldwide, we have been successful in guaranteeing spiritual follow-up and support for many. Today, a church aboard a ship is reality. That alone underscores the gravity and necessity of this work. The rights of God take precedence over all human rights. People everywhere need to hear the gospel and experience the effects. In numerous ports on every continent, and in the homes of friends of seafarers, those previously unreached men and women experience the love of God daily.

The ministry to seafarers has already borne fruit and its fruit will increase. This book calls our attention to an often forgotten and neglected area of missionary service. Its story will inspire readers to lend their support this very key missionary service.

Marco Gmür
Missiologist, Switzerland

Author's note

I am indebted to Marcy Schönke, an American living in Hamburg, for translating this book, which was originally written in German, into English. She has done a wonderful job.
I would also like to thank Mike Wilson, the Director of the Seamen's Christian Friend Society (SCFS), for reading the manuscript and offering very helpful comments.

For more information visit our website at
http://www.seafarers-ministry.de
or contact the author by e-mail at
scfs.martin.otto@t-online.de

Introduction

The ocean rages and roars, unlike anything the seafarers have experienced before. Huge waves roll over the ship. A seaman sent to check the security of the containers on deck is seized by a great wave and thrown into the sea. How terrifying! But the next wave throws him back on board. This African understands God's message . . .

Moses, the radio officer of his ship, is looking forward to being back home with his family. He is on his last journey which takes him through the perilous and dreaded Biscaya. Suddenly horror is written on the faces of the crew – the engines have broken down! And right in the midst of a wind-force of 12! The ship becomes a plaything for the waves. Twenty seafarers, among them Moses, lose their lives when the *River Guara* sinks . . .

Tables, chairs and dishes go flying through the air. The lifeboat is torn from its anchoring. Loud shouts are heard everywhere. The *River Adada* struggles in a desperate fight for survival. There's only one hope – prayer! Muslims as well as Christians plead to God for their lives. Everyone is saved and three Muslims convert to Christianity when they see how clearly God answers prayer . . .

Nightshift in the engine room. Suddenly the doors are thrown open! Heavily armed pirates climb aboard the ship, tie up the engineer and threaten to kill him after they have plundered the ship. An unexpected, loud machine alarm makes the pirates nervous and they flee. The engineer becomes a believer when he realizes that God heard his desperate prayer . . .

Fire alarm! The sirens wail and wail. Seafarers despairingly search the ship until they discover the cause – a fire in the engine room! In the darkness the men feel their way forward. The electric power supply has been destroyed by the fire. Suddenly they stumble over comrades who lie dead on the floor . . .

While going about their work at sea, some seafarers discover five Africans hiding in a loading hatch in an attempt to escape from West Africa and reach the 'golden West'. At the command of the captain the stowaways are cast into the sea. As they try to swim back to the ship, the crew shoots them. One African, who was not discovered, manages to reach Le Havre, France, and reports the incident to the police. The ship's officers are arrested, taken to court, and a few months later they are given sentences.

* * *

What kind of people are these, who year after year risk their lives at sea so that they may be able to feed their families? And who will seek them out in the many ports of the world and take the gospel of Jesus Christ to them? Seafarers are often a forgotten people; many Christians aren't even aware of their existence. Therefore, I have made it my goal through this book to inform and to urge people to bring the good news of Jesus Christ to these forgotten men and women. The seafarer's mission is a unique opportunity to meet lonely and abandoned people, sometimes eking out a miserable existence on ships. Who will go to them and bring them hope? Who will let them know that they are not alone? Who will help them with the very real cares of everyday life?

Since Old Testament times God has been calling us to speak of his wonders and to give him the glory – and that challenged me to do it by writing this book. Years ago some Christians suggested that it might be a good idea to write a book about the seafarers' mission – and now I have done it, solely for the sake of the glory of God.

My hope is that through this book people will be encouraged in their faith to trust in God, to single-mindedly follow him, to take the Great Commission of Jesus seriously and to ask themselves: 'Lord, where do you want me to serve you and tell others of the Good News?' It is also my desire that this book will show those interested in missions new possibilities for missionary service, and that many will be won for this special ministry.

Since this type of missionary work isn't very well known, and it doesn't seem that much has been written about it, I have decided to show the unique possibilities for missions among seafarers. Whenever I talk about this work at missions conferences or churches I often get reactions such as: 'I didn't even know that such a work existed. Please tell me more about it!'

Countless articles and books have already been written with the aim of encouraging Christians to become aware of and to reach out to the so-called 'unreached peoples'. Yet there are also many unreached people in our own countries and we hardly take notice of them. Very few of us know that seafarers are included in this group. We don't see them in our town, city or country. And we will hardly find them in our church since they spend their lives at sea.

Psalm 107:23–32 speaks of seafarers and their difficult circumstances:

> Others went out on the sea in ships,
> they were merchants on the mighty waters.
> They saw the works of the Lord,
> his wonderful deeds in the deep.
> For he spoke and stirred up a tempest
> that lifted high the waves.
> They mounted up to the heavens
> and went down to the depths;
> in their peril their courage melted away.
> They reeled and staggered like drunken men,
> they were at their wits' end.
> Then they cried out to the Lord in their trouble,
> and he brought them out of their distress.
> He stilled the storm to a whisper;
> the waves of the sea were hushed.
> They were glad when it grew calm,
> and he guided them to their desired haven.
> Let them give thanks to the Lord
> for his unfailing love
> and his wonderful deeds for men.
> Let them exalt him in the assembly of the people
> and praise him in the council of the elders.

It was Jesus who calmed the storm on the Lake of Gennesaret as we
see in Mark 4:37–41:

> A furious squall came up, and the waves broke over the boat, so
> that it was nearly swamped. Jesus was in the stern, sleeping on a
> cushion. The disciples woke him and said to him, 'Teacher, don't
> you care if we drown?' He got up, rebuked the wind and said to
> the waves, 'Quiet! Be still!' Then the wind died down and it was
> completely calm. He said to his disciples, 'Why are you so afraid?
> Do you still have no faith?' They were terrified and asked each
> other, 'Who is this? Even the wind and the waves obey him!'

Seafarers generally come from non-western countries and they
spend nine to twelve months on the ship, then two months at
home and again nine to twelve months back at sea. This means
that in thirty years the father of a family may be at home with his
family for a total of five years! These seamen arrive in our harbour
cities and feel alone, far away from their families. One can often
see them leaning over the ship's railing, just waiting for someone
to come and keep them company.

More than 1.2 million seafarers worldwide

According to an English company[1] that compiles data, figures
and facts about seafarers and ships, there were more than 1.2
million men and women working as seafarers in 1995 – these
figures have probably risen since then. Here in Hamburg my team
and I have already met seafarers from over one hundred different
countries. Many of them come from places in which missionaries
are not welcome, for example Islamic, Hindu or Buddhist
countries. However, on board ships we have the opportunity to
meet these people. They come to our port cities: here they are not
under pressure from religious authorities as they may be at home,
and so they are open to the gospel. When the Scriptures are put

---

[1] See on the Internet <http://www.marisec.org> the website of the
International Chamber of Shipping (ICS) and the International Shipping
Federation (ISF).

into their hands, God's word reaches the furthest and most isolated corners of the world. Even if they do not bring it into their homes, they have the chance to read the Bible and perhaps even come into contact with other Christians in other ports. Seafarers are often lonely and don't always have the possibility to leave their ship. Different nationalities frequently work together on board which leads to difficulties in communication. This special kind of loneliness makes them much more willing to read the Bible or watch the *Jesus* film[2] than they may have been at home. For Muslims, Buddhists and Hindus from fundamentalist countries, there is no better opportunity to accept the gospel than on a ship.

The current situation in the ports worldwide

It is unfortunate that this unique chance to evangelize has been neglected by churches and missionary societies in the last decades. For over two hundred years people have worked to win seafarers for Jesus Christ by visiting ships and inviting seafarers into their homes or churches. As early as 1779 there were reports about missionary work among seafarers by the Naval, Military and Air Force Bible Society in England which dedicated itself to this task. A book by Dr Kverndal[3] reports the history of missionary attempts to reach seafarers. Today there are full-time missionaries working in different ports around the world, but many more workers are still needed. The great ports of the world – Hong Kong, Singapore, Kaoshiung, Rotterdam, Shanghai, Tokyo, New York and Los Angeles – are in desperate need of more full-time workers who can bring the gospel to these lonely people.

The homepage of the website of the port of Hong Kong[4] states that between 100 and 200 ships anchor there daily. According to the International Transport Workers Federation (ITF) in London,

---

[2] A film about the life of Jesus according to the Gospel of Luke.

[3] R. Kverndal, *Seamen's Missions: Their Origins and Early Growth* (Pasadena, CA: William Carey Library, 1986).

[4] Website of the Hong Kong Government Marine Department <http://www.info.gov.hk/mardep>.

the Chinese government is undertaking to send thousands of Chinese men and women to language schools so that they will be able to work on international ships when their English is good enough.[5]

[5] Website of ITF <http://www.itf.org.uk>.

1

A People without a Home

Many think of seafarers as people who have made their hobby – travelling – into their profession. They travel around the whole world without having to buy one ticket. On the contrary – they get paid for it and on top of that they have a chance to see all of the beautiful places in all of the different countries of the world!

That is, of course, a very superficial way of looking at things. Seafarers experience something entirely different from what the landlubbers romantically imagine when they think of this type of occupation. Many seafarers have no roots and do not really

A Taiwanese ship shortly before berthing in Hamburg.

feel at home either in their own country or at sea. A survey carried out by the Seafarers' Union in 1996 among 6,000 seafarers revealed the following facts, which were included in a report that sheds light on the situation of many seafarers.

The age of seafarers and the length of their service
Sixty per cent of the persons asked were under the age of 40. The youngest group of seafarers (according to nationality) were the Filipinos and the Chinese. Half of those surveyed had been at sea for more than 10 years. Most of the seamen spent an average of six to twelve months at sea, two months at home and then several months separated from their families again. They literally sacrificed themselves for their families so that their children may have a better life than they have had and may achieve a higher standard of living.

The financial situation
The wages on board were often very low – 52 per cent said they earned less than $1,100 dollars each month. Twenty-three per cent of seafarers supported five or more persons back at home, while 55 per cent said they supported between two and four persons.

Communication
The days can be very lonely. One has to consider that communication among the seafarers is often hardly possible due to the fact that on some ships people from up to twelve different nationalities work together. Of those interviewed, 42 per cent worked on ships where they could not communicate in their native language and 11 per cent were totally dependent on translators for communication. Only 30 per cent worked on ships where one language was spoken.

The working day
Seafarers have to work under conditions that make their work both challenging and difficult. Storms and problems are constant companions. Just under 25 per cent of those interviewed said they worked eight hours or less a day; 62 per cent worked between eight and twelve hours; 11 per cent worked between 12 and 18 hours; and 3 per cent worked over 18 hours a day. On passenger ships, 33 per cent of the employees were on duty for over 12 hours a day.

Safety
A seafarer is constantly confronted with uncertainties and dangers. In fact, most of them had already been involved in some type of accident. Forty-four per cent answered that in the previous year they themselves had an accident. In addition to accidents there is the more serious risk of sinking. Every year ships go under, and the news doesn't even reach the press.

Cases of abuse
Twenty-five per cent of the seafarers answered that due to their nationality or race they had been subject to unfair treatment. Ten per cent disclosed that they had been beaten or physically maltreated.

Temptations
For many seamen shore leave is a temptation to become involved with women. Prostitutes work in most port cities and go aboard ship as well.

Finally back home
The real problems begin when the seaman arrives home! What awaits him when, after many lonely months at sea, he returns home and sees his family – the very people for whom he has made these sacrifices? During the first few days everyone is happy that the husband, or father, uncle, brother or nephew, is back home. Even the seaman himself accepts the fact that he is treated almost as a guest because, after all, he was away for almost a whole year. He is now the centre of attention. The souvenirs he has brought are all admired – things that most of his fellow countrymen only dream about.

But his happiness is dampened when he hears his children calling him 'Uncle' instead of 'Daddy', or when his smaller children shyly hide behind their mother, wondering whether they can trust this stranger. When he tries to take on the role of father and head of the family again, he discovers to his disappointment that neither his opinions or instructions nor advice are heeded. Everyone is used to having mother make the decisions that affect the family. This inevitably leads to conflict between the partners, since it is not easy to make such big role adjustments during the short time the father is at home on leave. The seaman finds himself in a dilemma. When he is at sea, he feels like a stranger; he is lonely and he misses his family. Now that he is home he makes the painful discovery that his family seems to get along quite well without him and he begins to long for his life on the ship. Very few men are able to break out of this vicious circle – and only with God's help is it possible.

* * *

Dr Erol Kahveci of Seafarers International Research Centre (SIRC) conducted more than one hundred detailed interviews with Filipino seafarers' wives. The study looked in depth at how families were affected, socially and financially, by their absent fathers. During the study, focus group discussions were also organized with seafarers' children to document their experiences. Twelve children were randomly selected and organized in three different groups according to their ages. The youngest child was 11 and the oldest one was 20.

It is known that the Filipinos is one of the most schooled nations in Asia. However, in comparison to the rest of the population, one of the striking characteristics of seafarers' children (aged between 7 and 21) is that they are overwhelmingly in full-time education. They also tend to study at private schools. As well as contributing to the social and cultural infrastructure of Filipino society this puts the seafarers' children in a better position as far as their future prospects are concerned, especially employment prospects.

When seafarers' children were asked to highlight the advantages of having seafarer fathers – apart from better education opportunities – they highlighted a number of things. One 15-year-old girl said: 'You can easily ask for money from him.' Other comments which highlight the positive side of being a seafarer's child included 'He can tell us about the other countries'; 'I think seafaring is very good for money, and when my father arrives we can eat lots of chocolate'; 'For me the advantage is we can get things like nice clothes and everything we need'; 'I can appreciate the things that my dad gives me, like new shoes, but then happiness is not all about material things. If you share some fun it's totally different, because it never ends. It will always be with you, not like shoes that will be disposed of.'

As the statements above suggest, however, the needs of seafarers' children go well beyond material things. In fact some children see the gifts as the result of their fathers' guilty consciences. 'I think for my father the idea of giving presents is a mechanism for coping with the time that he has not been with us,' said one 19-year-old son. A seafarer's daughter made a similar point: 'I think when my father tries to give us presents when he gets home it is his way of trying to compensate for all those times that he wasn't there for us. Although he says it's his present, there's that feeling deep inside that he's really trying to compensate for all those lost times.'

The memories of 'those lost times' and of their father's absence during their childhood remain with the children for a long time. They particularly recollect the memories attached to special days, such as birthdays, Christmas Day, degree ceremonies and other personal achievements. This is what one girl said: 'It's basically those special days, such as when you achieve something, and then you really want to share your achievement with your family. But then you know there's one member in your family who can't attend, who can't share your happiness. It's just that there are times when you feel you need your father the most. It's those times that he's away.'

The lengthy absences of seafarers from their children also have adverse effects on paternal bonding. As one child put it: 'The bond has been broken ever since my early childhood. We never talked, he never shared opinions, we never shared ideas or anything.' Another girl had this to say: 'I just get used to the idea of my father being away. I was a little kid when he went, so maybe that's why I just get used to it. I miss him and send letters sometimes.'

Without any exception, all the children say that having their father at home makes them feel more secure and the family complete. However, adjustment to the fathers' arrival is not a smooth process, as the children explain: 'Most of the time I feel like we are one of his men on the ship. There are times he keeps on saying "You have to finish this at this time" and "You have to do this before that." There are lots of commands.'

'We have to wake early because my dad wants us to wake up when he is up. He doesn't want us to sit down and relax, he wants us to do things. He wants all the family working and working and working. Maybe he's used to the ship. When he's on the ship everybody's working.'

As these comments suggest, seafarers' leave period brings mixed feelings for their children – feelings that move between feeling 'more secure and complete' to being 'under command'. The children also expressed the negative side of their fathers' arrival home in relation to financial matters. As one child explains: 'Mostly my mother and father argue about money, why there aren't any savings and also why we kids spend so much money.'

The children are appreciative and aware of their fathers' hard-earned money. However, being reminded of it all the time has negative effects. It makes them feel that they're a burden to their families. As one girl explains: 'In the first semester I failed in two subjects and that makes me hate myself because I wanted to prove to my dad that his money is worth something. So then I feel I am a burden to my family. I've wasted some of my dad's money and I hate it.'

Another child, a boy, had something similar to say: 'In my first year I was having a hard time adjusting to college life and after I had seen my grades I thought that I was just a burden on the family. I haven't shown anything of worth, and that's the reason why I have changed my course. Now I am studying hotel and restaurant management which is much cheaper.'

During a typical seafarer's contract of nine months great physical and emotional changes can take place in a young child's life, and seafarers' children frequently expressed concerns about their fathers' lack of recognition of these changes. One teenage girl said: 'When our fathers come home they expect us to still be the little kids they left behind. Things change, but they think nothing changes because it is fixed in their minds that we're still the young ones they loved before. Sometimes there are many misunderstandings because our fathers are not with us for a year, or sometimes for two years. They cannot understand that when they're away we change. They want us to be what we were before, and sometimes they cannot accept the fact that we are what we are.'

* * *

As part of another project, researchers from SIRC have spent almost three hundred days at sea sailing with seafarers on 14 different ships. During the interviews with seafarers it became clear that one of the main reasons that seafarers like their jobs is that they can support their families and provide a better future for their children. The majority of the seafarers also expressed strongly that they do not like being away from their families.

Seafarers are rightly proud of what they achieve for their children. However, as some of the comments from their children suggest, there are certain problems that the children encounter because of the lengthy absences of their fathers. The aim of this section is not to paint a pessimistic picture of seafarers' family life but to give a voice to their children, as part of seeking solutions to their problems. Perhaps the first step forward comes from the children themselves: 'My dad spends a lot of time away from us because of his job, so communication really matters. If we communicated better all problems would be talked through. By communicating we could understand why we have these kinds of problems. That way it would not be hard for me and my dad to understand each other.'[6]

The seafarers' absence can also present problems for their wives. Mrs Clarita Samar has written: 'During his vacation, he spent all the days except Sunday on training and seminars. And if I may say so, he hasn't spent it with us, his family. Although I know that all of these training days and seminars are requirements for his position, I feel it's not fair that he goes on board for six months and then has his training here for three months. We will survive, though, because we have faith and hope that God will end all our longing and hardship and in time we will live as one whole family.'

Here is what Myrna Ferriol Virtudazo, a Filipino wife of a seaman, had to say about the arrival of her husband:

> His homecoming is like a honeymoon. How intoxicating and joyful! Everybody is on cloud nine. The wife is on top of the world. The husband is overflowing with love and attention. The

---

[6] Reproduced with kind permission of Dr Erol Kahveci from the Seafarers International Research Centre, Cardiff, UK.

children are overwhelmed by Dad's generosity. You are ready to forgive the hurts, which were inflicted upon you.

When the honeymoon period is over, how difficult everything becomes! Everybody comes back down to earth. The wife takes the back seat. The husband is beset with disillusionments and becomes demanding. The children are wary and confused by Dad's moods, which can switch – sunny one minute and critical the next. Once more you are harbouring the hurts that you thought were already buried. After twenty-one years of married life and six children, I would say that I have encountered some dilemmas as a seafarer's wife. I bet he has too, although in a different way.

My husband, who was the eldest in the family and the first to earn a living abroad (being a seafarer) is a good son and brother. I thought that he would make a good husband and father. And he did. The trouble was, I was not prepared to take the great responsibility of having to take care of his brothers and sisters, who lived with us under one roof during the crucial early stages of our married life. I could not bear the task that was suddenly heaped on my lap, not to mention having to cope with different characters, habits and upbringing. It was like heavy baggage that threw me to the ground.

I could not write about the pain I had been going through, because I did not want him to worry, and his job might be affected. I could not discuss it either when he was on vacation, because I did not want to ruin his precious moments with us.

The change came when I came into a personal relationship with the Lord Jesus Christ. Slowly I learned to trust in Christ despite the many problems. I learned to tell Jesus all my sorrows and problems, and healing started to take place. Soon after Jesus changed me, my husband also came to know Jesus. When my husband comes home now, we take time in prayer and spend our time together with God's help.[7]

---

[7] Published in the Filipino newspaper *Tinig ng Marino*, September 1997.

2

Unexpected Opportunities

Almost daily we encounter seafarers who are open to the gospel. The literature we distribute isn't just quickly glanced at and then thrown away, as often happens in many western countries. On the contrary, it is usually read very carefully. At the beginning of my time as a missionary I often wondered how God would use the literature (tracts, Bibles, cassettes, videos, Christian posters, leaflets, etc.). To my amazement, God often did much more than I, with my small faith, ever thought possible. During those first years I could hardly believe my eyes when I saw how someone would immediately read through the whole tract or booklet, even when it was twenty pages long. And I remember sometimes being discouraged when I was 'only' able to distribute literature because the seafarers were too busy and couldn't take a break. But I once received a long letter from a Polish woman who wrote the following: 'You gave my father a tract when he was working on a ship in Hamburg. He passed it on to me. I read it and came to recognize that I was separated from God because of my sins, and I prayed to receive Jesus into my life. I only have a New Testament. Do you think you could send me a whole Bible?' I was more than happy to fulfil her wish!

A Russian seafarer once wrote that he read the tract *A Letter For You*, which we had distributed on his ship. When he had finished, he prayed to receive Jesus Christ as Lord, and he was so excited that he gave the tract to one of his comrades. This annoyed his colleague who put it aside, but then later on he did read it. Now this man came to faith in Jesus. When those two seafarers finished their time on the ship and returned home, they both looked for a church to join and wrote, 'Please tell us how we can now best serve in our church?'

This greatly encouraged me to keep handing out literature. Before the time of President Gorbachev there was a great deal of interest in Christian literature on Russian ships. But whenever I boarded a Russian ship, the political officers tried to keep an eye on me, which didn't make it easy to bring material on board. I would then ask to speak to the captain so that the officer would think I was there to talk about business.

In spite of these difficulties it was sometimes possible for me to start up a conversation with a seafarer. Once the second officer invited me into his cabin and begged me to give him any literature I had. He then proceeded to hide it. He told me: 'If I'm caught with these things I'll not only lose my job but I'll also be sent to prison, and my wife and children will also get into trouble.' As I was leaving the ship, I asked the officer on duty if he'd like to have a Bible and he coldly answered 'No!' I had almost reached the gangway[8] when that same officer suddenly whispered to me, 'Hey, give me a Bible!' I ran to him, he opened his coat and quickly hid the Bible inside.

After the fall of the Soviet Union, people often asked me for Bibles. I often heard the question: 'Have you got a Bible for me?' When Russian seamen saw me coming they would surround my car and the only thing they would say to me was: 'Bible!' I then took whatever material I had and passed out tracts, cassettes and Bibles, as well as children's Bibles.

At one point I became suspicious and thought, 'What are they doing with all this literature? Are they selling it because they're so poor?' So, on one occasion I went back to the ship and had a look around. I looked into the engine room and saw the third engineer; he was supposed to be working but instead he was reading a Bible. After that I went to the bridge, quietly opened the door and saw the same thing: the captain was reading the Bible.

The situation is similar on Chinese ships today. One also finds political officers there who are in charge of keeping watch over the crew. In order to show proper respect towards the authority on board, I always go straight to the captain when I visit a ship. I have found that if I have something to hand out, that is the best

---

[8] A ramp or stairway leading to the ship.

place to begin anyway. In addition, it is always important to get permission before distributing literature on communist ships.

Once I was on a Chinese ship drinking tea with the captain and a few other crew members. When I tried to present them with some of my literature, the captain declined with a wave of his hand. In this way he let me know I should not try anymore. Shortly afterwards one of the crew members left the room. I later found out that he was the political officer. As soon as this man disappeared the captain asked me for a Chinese Bible. He then hid it behind the curtain and said, 'No one should know what I've just put here.'

Fortunately it is now getting easier to distribute material on Chinese ships. Aboard another ship I once crossed paths with an ordinary seaman, and without even having exchanged a word with him, I just handed him a Bible. The moment he recognized what it was, tears began streaming down his cheeks. That puzzled me and I wondered if I'd made some sort of cultural blunder. So I asked him, and he reassured me that I hadn't done anything wrong. What made him cry was that it was the first Bible he'd ever had in his life. Now he wanted to begin reading it.

He read the Bible daily for several weeks. After his ship left Hamburg, I wrote to him and he answered back:

Dear Martin,

It was a great surprise to receive your letter and the books you sent. Thank you. I have read your letter several times through. My friend, do you know, I am now a born-again Christian, a new man. Jesus gave his life for me and saved me with his blood! I have no reason to doubt his great love and kindness. I trust him entirely and look to him as my Saviour. Every morning and evening I pray to God, because he has forgiven my sins and put joy in my heart. When I read Rev. 3:20 I was very moved by Jesus' love for me. He is willing to come to anyone who accepts him. I have read in John 1:12 that if I accept Jesus, he will make me his child. By the way, I have worked through the Bible correspondence course and am sending you the answer sheet. My friend, you showed me the way. I will never forget you. I will always remember our meeting on the ship.

Your friend, Sun Jian

While I was visiting the *Queen Elizabeth II*, probably the most well-known passenger ship in the world, a seafarer told me about a problem they had. There was already a group of believers who met for fellowship on board, but since they came from different denominations[9] it was difficult for them to do any systematic study of the Bible.

He explained to me that they needed someone who could teach them God's word, and he asked me to come and teach them during the time that the ship was in dry dock. I gladly accepted the invitation and met with the group on Wednesday evenings. One year later I was surprised and delighted to learn from our seafarer's missionary in Southampton (England) that, as a result of my teaching, nine seafarers had accepted Jesus as their Saviour and rededicated their lives to him.

When the seafarers spend many months at sea there's little they can do in their free time after they have finished their work. It gets especially boring while the ship is on the high seas, where life is not as hectic as in the ports. I often hear from seafarers that they are happy to be able to listen to good music or see a good film. After a few weeks everyone has seen all the films that there are on board, so when I bring them the *Jesus* film they look forward to watching it. Several seafarers have told me that they watch the *Jesus* film every Sunday.

One evening, when a crew was planning to go and visit the red light district[10] of Hamburg, I told them that there was something even better they could do. I gave them the *Jesus* film, and the whole crew remained on the ship to watch it. In fact, they watched it twice, from start to finish! This gave them the opportunity to think about the life of Jesus for four hours.

One morning in December 2000 I arrived on a small German tanker. I didn't have a clue that a seaman had already prayed to God asking that someone would come and show him the way of salvation. I met Lemon in the mess room[11] while having a cup of coffee. As I began to explain the gospel to him, he seemed to be

---

[9] Religious groups from the same faith that have slightly different beliefs.
[10] An area of a city where night clubs and brothels are usually located.
[11] The dining hall of the ship.

very interested, so I encouraged him to do a Bible corres-pondence course. He agreed.

The next time we met he had a few questions for me. Then, after the third lesson of the course, Lemon felt Jesus speaking to his heart and he offered a prayer of surrender. We met again and he told me the following story: 'I got food poisoning from some mussels, and I was so sick that I didn't think I'd survive. I prayed to Jesus at this time and said "Jesus, if you let me die now, what meaning did my life have? Up to now I have only lived for myself, without honouring you. Please give me a chance and send me someone who can show me the way to you."' A few days later I happened to visit the ship and Lemon's prayer was answered. Now he is back home in the Philippines on leave and he has made it his goal to tell his relatives about the changes in his life.

Perhaps one of the best things about being on a ship is that seamen are able to concentrate on the Bible more easily than they otherwise might do. Back at home there are so many things competing for their attention. For example, they are busy with family matters. Or they are working on their houses. They might even be studying for

An iron-ore carrier with Filipino crew.

their officer's exams. When their leave is over and they have returned to the ship they are alone again; they start thinking about the problems they couldn't solve at home and these things occupy their thoughts. So it is no surprise that in this situation many seamen begin to think about the meaning of life as well as eternity. In the back of many minds there is also the fear that they may never return home safely and see their loved ones again.

Once, on a Greek ship, I met with a large group of Muslims from Asia who listened as I was talking about the life-changing power of Jesus. We were sitting in the mess room talking and several of the men asked me for Bibles. Afterwards one man came up to me and told me that, although he was a Muslim, Jesus had healed him from an illness when a missionary prayed for him while he was in Japan.

We often come into contact with people who are Hindu, Buddhist, Muslim or Christian in name only. Yet they have deep questions and are searching for answers. When we meet them and they are alone, with no one observing them, they feel free to talk about Jesus. At present Muslim seafarers on the ships are especially open and willing to listen to the message of the gospel and discuss it with us.

We also experience a great deal of openness among the seafarers from countries like China. Sometimes Chinese people ask us for Christian literature to take back to their families, relatives, friends and churches. I am often asked for a Bible – the Chinese call it the 'big book'. One man who was so happy to receive a Bible wrote to me:

> Dear Mr Otto,
>
> I thank you very much for helping me to believe in Jesus Christ, God's Son. Every day I now read the Bible you gave me. The stories in it are so interesting. I have also read the tract, *A Letter For You,* and I am trying to understand what's written in it. There's one sentence in it that I will never forget: 'For God so loved the world that he gave his only begotten Son, that whoever believes in him shall not perish, but have eternal life.' Please teach me more about God and about the history of Israel. I wait every day to hear from you.
>
> Your spiritual son, a Christian, Yang Hai Dong

It is through seafarers that we often have the opportunity to pass God's word on to people from places we would not normally encounter. Again and again we meet seafarers who ask us to give them Bibles, books, videos and Bible correspondence courses for their wives, children and friends. One man wrote to us with the request that, when he arrives in Hamburg, we should set aside twenty to thirty Bibles for him because he needs them for his church. Other seafarers write asking me for books such as concordances[12] – for their pastors in their home country.

Fellowship is vital to seafarers, no matter whether they are Christians or not. Many seafarers are very lonely and they need someone to talk with as well as someone who is simply willing to listen. Some have told me how much they appreciated just being able to talk to me about everyday things. One man from Nigeria told me that he had sent me a total of six letters from different ports in the world, but never got an answer. When we finally met and I told him that I hadn't received any of the letters, he said: 'Today God has healed my soul. I was beginning to have doubts about being a Christian.' Fellowship means very much, since the seafarers are at sea for two, three or even up to six weeks without having contact with other people.

As I mentioned before, through friendships with seafarers God's word is passed on to others. When a seafarer is home he often tells his family and friends all about the people he has met on his journeys. We have received letters from wives, telling us how happy and thankful they were that their husbands had a friend. That is a wonderful way to win the whole family.

Another means of building friendships and having fellowship is through letters. Sometimes seafarers whom I have never met write to me. They have found my address and they simply begin to write, telling me about everyday things, problems they have, or they request a Bible correspondence course, or they are simply seeking friendship. In this way I have been corresponding with some seafarers for many years.

One officer I visited and to whom I later wrote, answered me promptly:

---

[12] A reference book for the Bible.

I have received your inspiring letter as well as the picture of your family. Your letter and the picture meant a lot to me and so I sent them on to my family because I wanted them to see who my new friend is. I know it will make them very happy, because I have told them all about you. How I would love to be able to visit you in your home and meet your family, but until now work on the ship has always made it impossible. I would like to tell you about a spiritual problem of mine. I am not strong enough to resist the temptations on the ship. I always pray to God that he will give me the strength I need, because I don't want to give into temptation and then feel separated from God. I want to grow from a spiritual baby into a mature spiritual adult. For that reason I was very happy when you gave me the Bible correspondence course. These courses help me very much. Someday, when I become captain, I hope to share God's word with other seafarers. I would like to give Bible studies and be an example to others, as to how one can resist temptation.

Sometimes God leads in ways that are different from how we would have done things. One evening, around 8 o'clock, I was getting ready to go home when I sensed that I should go and visit a certain ship. I thought that it was a bit late and that maybe I should just visit that ship another time. Yet, somehow that inner voice didn't let up, and I felt that God wanted to have me on that ship. So I drove to where the ship was docked and went to the guard, who told me that the ship would be leaving in about half an hour's time. Now that confused me a bit and I thought that perhaps I hadn't really heard God's voice. I went on board and met a few drunken men playing cards, which made me even more unsure of myself. When I finally knocked on another cabin door, someone said, 'Come in.' I had hardly sat down when the seaman, a Filipino, asked me for a Bible in Tagalog, the language of the Philippines. After a short conversation it was time to leave the ship. Several weeks later I received a letter from this man who told me that he had found Jesus. A crucial factor for him had been the possibility to read the Bible in his native language.

I often recognize God's leading in certain situations only weeks or months afterwards. It is wonderful to know that God always has a broad perspective of things and does everything in his own time.

When I was on a Ro-Ro ship[13] talking to the men about the gospel during lunchtime I didn't get many reactions. A while later though, a seafarer from Ghana came up to me and told me that what he'd heard had moved him. He said, 'I still have a few questions. Would you maybe have time for me, to answer my questions?' We sat down together a few times after that and read the Bible together, and I was able to explain to him the way of salvation. When all of his questions had been answered, he wanted to receive Jesus into his life. It was a special joy for me to see him from time to time over the next few years and to accompany him in his faith.

As much as we love to see people come to Christ, it is also important to encourage Christians who are feeling lonely. I once met a Christian by the name of Tafesse, who came from Ethiopia. He told me that in Ethiopia he had spent three years in prison because of his belief in Jesus Christ. 'But,' he added, 'the prison wasn't nearly as a bad as this ship where I am now working. In prison I was allowed to receive visitors. Here I am alone and people make fun of me because of my faith.' We prayed that he would no longer be the only Christian on board. The next time I visited the ship there were two other believers from Ethiopia working there, and they met together with Tafesse for daily prayer and fellowship around God's word.

During the coffee break on a small grain ship I once met some seafarers from Kiribati and the Philippines. One of the men from Kiribati asked me to help him buy a tennis racket. I wasn't really interested in doing anything like that, but I had the feeling I should, so we went shopping. When we returned, this man told all of the other seamen how much I had helped him, and suddenly I was surrounded by a crowd of men, looking at me. My friend then told me: 'Tell the officer about Jesus.' So I promptly called all of the men into the crew's quarters and explained the gospel to them. The second officer was there and I noticed he had tears in his eyes. He told me that some of his relatives were believers

---

[13] A ship that is loaded and unloaded by means of a ramp at the stern. Therefore it is known as a 'roll on, roll off' ship.

and that he himself had begun reading the Bible. Four seafarers asked me for a Bible correspondence course so that they could become familiar with the Bible.

During my visit to a bulk carrier[14] someone asked me how a telephone card works, which I explained to him. After that the crew, consisting of men from Rumania, Bulgaria and Turkey, noticed I had Bibles with me and eight of the men requested a Bible in their language. One Muslim seafarer then asked: 'Which gospel do I have to believe: the gospel of Matthew, Mark, Luke or John?'

Hamburg is also increasingly becoming a port for passenger ships. In 2001 around 35 cruise ships anchored in Hamburg. In 2002 the number should rise to 66. The main difference for me and my work on these ships is that, unlike the container ships where approximately 20 seafarers usually work, cruise ships can have hundreds of people from many different countries working on them. I have been able to distribute literature on two cruise ships, *Radiance of the Seas* and *Black Watch*. The *Radiance of the Seas*, for example, has nine hundred people working on board. On both ships, while on board, I prayed that God would lead me to people who were prepared. On the first ship I met the manager of the crew who invited me to hold a Bible study one evening. At that meeting there were fifteen people from eight different countries. On the second ship I was also able to hold a meeting that was attended by seafarers from the Philippines, Cuba and Indonesia. A Muslim seafarer who was present said: 'Actually I am not allowed to attend this Bible study, but I am interested.' When I visited the ship the next day, the same man asked me, 'Can you come again this evening and lead another Bible study for us?'

We want to take advantage of the opportunities on freight and passenger ships, so that people will find out about Jesus and churches may be planted.

---

[14] A ship which only carries a certain type of cargo, e.g. coal, grain, iron ore. These are stored in individual compartments or hatches and are called bulk goods.

3

Difficulties and Disappointments

Those who work with seafarers over a period of time find that there are a lot of difficulties and problems, which have no easy solutions. Not only that, disappointments and frustrations are things one just has to learn to live with. Whoever expects a missionary to work without problems is simply not being realistic. Ephesians 6 tells us that we are in a spiritual battle; we are not dealing with flesh and blood, but rather our struggle is against the rulers and authorities, against the powers of this dark world and spiritual forces of evil. It is true, they have been defeated through the death and resurrection of Jesus Christ. Nevertheless, I have felt this battle in my own life.

One ordinary day I was in the harbour visiting different ships, sharing the word of God with the seafarers. On my way home, my wife paged me so I stopped at the nearest telephone booth and called home to see if everything was okay. 'Not at all!' Monika replied. She continued, 'Someone just called and gave me a false name. After talking for a few minutes the caller said, "I am going to kill your husband!"' We were shocked! Who in the world wanted to do that? We couldn't imagine who it could be because we weren't having problems with anybody. However, around that time we had been getting a number of strange calls that made us feel extremely uneasy. Either the caller wouldn't identify himself or he would just call and swear at us. It really comforted us to know that many friends were praying for us. The calls finally stopped. Through it all, however, we could see that we were in a spiritual battle – which continues up to this day. Satan doesn't like it when we preach the good news of Jesus to seafarers every day.

Not long after these calls we had another shocking experience. I was in my car at a container port, waiting at the container terminal because a few vehicles in front of me were stacking containers.[15] While I was sitting there, a so-called van carrier[16] suddenly rammed into my car and completely destroyed it. Shaken but unhurt I got out, very thankful to God that the driver rammed into the passenger side of my car and not the side where I was sitting!

A similar incident happened to my colleague, Volker Lamaack, who was at the port and on his way to visit a ship. There is constant activity at the port and many things happen that make it a hazardous place. While he was driving around there, all of the sudden a forklift truck came out of a shed with its fork raised, and it drove into Volker's car. We were glad that the car was only badly dented and that Volker was able to escape unhurt.

Further to these two serious incidents we were involved in three more. We decided to ask friends always to pray for us, that we may safely reach the ships in the harbour and make it back home again. These accidents, as well as the death threats, made us realize that we only live by the grace of God. We are so grateful for the many friends who pray for us and in this way give us valuable support.

One of the difficulties we had, especially at the beginning of our work, was communication. We had (and still have) language problems almost every day. Fortunately many seafarers speak good English. Still, there are quite a few who only speak their native language and then we are forced to resort to gestures in order to communicate with each other. It is a great help to have God's word in almost every language that we find on the ships. Even when we can speak with people in English, however, it is sometimes difficult to understand the accent of the seafarer. There are great differences between the accents, for example, of a person from India and a person from Africa.

The culture can be even harder to understand than the language. During the first years of our missionary work I made hundreds of mistakes. For example, I once told a Filipino to his face that it would be wrong to pray the rosary. He was so insulted that he angrily jumped up and wanted to strangle me. Fortunately, several of his fellow Filipinos were also there and they were able to calm him

---

[15] A huge metal box which can be carried on trucks, trains or ships.

[16] A special vehicle for carrying containers.

A Chinese ship brings container bridges for a newly built port in Hamburg.

down. From this and other experiences I learned that with Filipinos I should always approach certain things in an indirect way, while at the same time not making any compromises regarding the gospel.

With seafarers from West Africa I have learned to at least taste the food set in front of me even if I don't eat it all. I think back to the time when I visited a ship from Nigeria and was offered some food. I politely declined but thanked the person for his hospitality. That evening we had some guests from the ship with us at home, and the main topic of our conversation was my refusal of the food offered to me that day. My guests explained to me that when I had refused the food I had hurt the cook's feelings and he felt personally rejected by me. So I had to get used to eating things even if I didn't like it. On one bulk carrier I was once served dog meat, which of course I ate. Fortunately I didn't know it was dog meat until afterwards.

Another potential area of friction is the radically different understanding of time from our understanding of it in western culture. I have often made appointments with seafarers to take

Seafarers!

them to Bible studies at church or to our home in the evening. We set the time and agreed on a meeting point. I arrived there and waited, but the seafarer didn't show up. When I later asked why the person didn't come, his answer puzzled me.

That was until I understood that culture plays a large role in dealing with invitations: in some cultures it is impolite to say no. It seemed that when I invited a seafarer and set an exact time to meet him, he didn't have the heart to refuse my invitation because he thought he would disappoint me. So he accepted the invitation in order to please me, but didn't show up at our meeting point. In a sense it caused me a lot of wasted time as well as mileage. But through it all I learned the importance of patience and of becoming familiar with different cultures.

It was often disappointing for me when there was a seafarer who hadn't been a Christian for very long on board a ship, which docked in Hamburg only for a few hours. In 1987, a few weeks after I had led Mariano Damaso, a Filipino, to Christ, I was told that his ship would be arriving in Hamburg one evening around 9 o'clock. So there I was, on the berth, but no ship in sight. The next morning I got up at dawn and rushed to the pier only to hear from a dockworker that the ship had already sailed. It had arrived at 11 o'clock and left Hamburg at 4 o'clock the next morning! I was so frustrated and didn't understand God! Didn't he know that a 'baby in the faith' was on board that ship? Naturally God knew that, but he wasn't dependent on me; he had other ways of taking care of his children. Yet that doesn't mean we should neglect follow-up work.

After 15 years of working among seafarers I see that God has had to teach me one lesson after another, for example, about the meaning of time in different cultures or about different situations on the ships. I often pray in the morning during my devotions that God will lead me to seafarers whose hearts are open to him.

* * *

Several years ago, after my quiet time in the morning, I picked out four ships to visit, packed my bag with literature to distribute and drove off to the first ship's berth. To my surprise the ship wasn't there. I thought to myself, 'Well, I'll just go to the next ship.' At the next pier the ship wasn't there either! At this moment, frustration and disappointment started welling up inside me. Questions shot through my head: 'Have I really heard God's voice or are these just my own ideas? Am I only going to the ships where I expect to be successful? Is there sin in my life that is keeping me from recognizing God's will? How can I give testimony to people when I don't even recognize his leading?' Gnawing questions and doubts. I finally decided to drive to the third pier where a ship was supposed to be. Once again the same thing – no ship! I parked my car and was overcome with despair. What should I do now? How was I supposed to recognize God's leading? Of course there's no schedule that falls from heaven, which shows where each ship is anchored.

As I sat there in my car, lost in thought, I suddenly noticed a red chimney: it belonged to a ship I hadn't seen until just then. I thought to myself, 'Well before I waste anymore time driving around the harbour, I'd just better go to a ship which is really anchored there.' After about 15 minutes I reached the ship and asked which nationalities were on board. They told me: 'Burma, India, China and the Philippines.' Then I got literature in the languages I needed and distributed it to the seafarers who happened to come my way. After that I went to the captain to introduce myself. He didn't seem to have any time because he was busy talking with some officers, but he asked me to wait outside his office.

After a few minutes he called me in and we were alone. I came straight to the point and explained why I was on board. I told him that I would like to talk with him about Jesus Christ. He signalled his interest so I began to explain the gospel. At one point he asked me if I had a Bible for him containing both the Old and New Testaments in his language, because he had wanted one for a long time. When I handed him one in Tagalog, he was overjoyed and we continued talking about faith in Jesus. It turned out to be a very, very long talk and in the end he asked me to come with him into his cabin. There we kneeled down and he surrendered his life to Jesus. The next day I visited the ship again in order to talk more with the captain about questions of faith. While I was there I heard that the ship was going to sail very soon, and actually the captain didn't have any time. But his new-found faith in Jesus had fascinated him so much that he just wanted to find out more.

Bringing our decisions into harmony with God's will is a problem we encounter on a daily basis. I often pray that God will show me his will but don't seem to receive an answer. Then I have the impression that God is trying to tell me, 'Make your decisions yourself, but don't forget me, and remain in close fellowship with me so that I can correct you when something doesn't go well.'

It sometimes seems that God gives us a great deal of autonomy. For example, I often go to a ship and have a strong feeling that God wants me to be there. Then I go to the recreation room during the afternoon coffee break at 3 o'clock and just wait, full of excitement, to see what God will do. Suddenly I realize that 10 minutes have passed and there's not a person in sight. Uncertainty and impatience creep up on me. And then questions like 'Am I wasting my time?' or 'Am I really sure I'm on the right ship?' fill my thoughts. Once I was waiting like that on the ship *Widar*, which regularly came to Hamburg. I was still waiting at 3:20. I began to think that it was not very effective to be waiting twenty minutes for nothing. I could have long been on another ship, sharing God's word with others. So I decided to leave. But, as I was getting ready to go I had the impression that the Holy Spirit was pressing me to stay. I stayed and continued to wait. At 3:30 I started to think about leaving. Finally at 3:35 a few Filipinos came in. One asked me right out if I had a Bible for him. I gave him one and he began to read it immediately.

When this man came back to Hamburg four weeks later, he asked me to explain to him what John 3:3 meant. In those four weeks he had read the first three gospels and now he had come to the subject of new birth. What did that mean – to be born again? So we made an appointment for the evening and I was able to sit with him for an hour and a half and teach him from the Scriptures. At the end of our time together this seafarer, Modival, had a desire to get right with God. Once again God's timing was perfect! On that day, if I hadn't stayed and waited, I would never have met this seafarer who was searching for the truth.

On another ship, while I was sitting in the crew's quarters, a seafarer came in and offered me a cup of coffee. Thanking him, I accepted his offer. But after he brought me the coffee he disappeared and there I was, alone with my hot coffee. I asked myself whether this was what a seafarer's missionary was supposed to do, drink coffee and just while away the time. When I had finished my coffee and was getting ready to go, another seafarer came in and asked me directly: 'Are you a Christian? Are you from the seamen's mission?' When I told him yes, he explained to me that he was the only Christian on board and that the day before he had prayed that on this day he would meet a Christian. His prayer was now answered.

Passenger ships are always a great challenge. On some of them there are a thousand people working of various nationalities. Since seafarers on these ships work longer hours than on freight ships they seldom have the opportunity to go on land, so they are very happy when we visit them and bring them God's word. I have often been able to teach weekly Bible classes on such passenger ships. Some of the seafarers have accepted Jesus as their Saviour. Yet it is always frustrating for us when the officers on duty don't give us the permission to go on board. Most of the time we are pretty sure that there are Christians on the ship who would love to have fellowship, and who need to be strengthened in their faith.

We are sometimes disappointed when our talks go in a totally different direction from what we'd hoped for, or when we don't have any talks at all. After all, we want to share the gospel with people. At the beginning of my missionary work it sometimes happened that I would visit a ship without a chance to talk with anyone. Either I didn't run into any seafarers or the ones I met weren't interested in talking about the gospel. What then? In such cases it becomes quite clear what one really depends on: successful talks or Jesus Christ. It shows whether one is focused on one's service or focused on Christ.

During one such a period, when I was driving through the port and plagued by many questions, God's gentle voice suddenly spoke to my heart: 'Martin are you willing to go your whole life without having any talks with people, just distributing tracts and Bibles and being faithful to me? Are you willing to continue the work without any visible success?' I gulped. I was shocked! Wasn't it God's intention for people to believe in Jesus? What would I say to churches when I was invited to missionary events? How could I say that I spent the whole day, the whole week, the whole month just distributing tracts?

But the questions God was asking me were unmistakably clear: 'Are you willing to walk in my way, carry out my plans, live to my glory, even if it means that nobody sees what you are doing?' As I sat there in my car feeling numb I understood what God meant. Nothing depends on me; everything we are and everything we do comes from God alone! I understood the message the Holy Spirit was trying to get across and I answered with tears in my eyes, 'Yes, Lord, I want to be willing. I want to be willing to do exactly what you want, no matter whether people see me or not. I only want to live for your glory.' Tears streamed down my face as I prayed, but a deep joy filled my heart. I knew this was a very decisive moment in my life.

How thankful I am for God's clear message to me because it helps me in everyday situations not to be focused on success but rather to live for Christ. Of course, there is still the danger of falling back into old habits. But it is good to know that the peace of God comes when we live for his glory. And that's just what I want to do.

It is sometimes disappointing when the seafarers fail to keep in touch with us while they are in their home country. There are many reasons for this. For example, sometimes seafarers aren't used to writing letters, or perhaps they feel inferior to the white western missionary. It can even happen that they have become caught up in some sin and are ashamed and afraid that the missionary will find out about it. Such are some of the experiences we've had in the past 15 years.

How wonderful it is, though, when we finally receive news from them. Once the nephew of a Filipino seafarer I had led to the faith wrote to me telling me that his uncle had come home a changed man. He wrote that they spent a lot of time together and that they regularly went to church. The nephew was so impressed by the transformation in his uncle that he asked me to send him a Bible correspondence course.

There was a married couple whom we had led to the faith at the beginning of our ministry; soon afterwards they returned to their country. We heard nothing from them, either by letter or telephone. After some time I met another Christian on a ship who had some news about this couple. He said that they had been baptized and that they were now faithfully serving in their church. God shows us through experiences like these that the seed that has been sown really does take root and grow.

Once, when I was on a Russian ship, I had the chance to distribute many New Testaments and Bibles while below deck. People were just grabbing things out of my hands. When everything was gone and the seafarers had returned to their work, one man grabbed hold of me and tried to push me behind an iron door and lock me in. I was afraid because I didn't know what could happen below deck. I finally managed to get out of his grip and run away. Fortunately the man didn't try to follow me and I escaped. Back in my car, with my knees shaking, I realized that things weren't always going to go smoothly. In spite of that, I could be sure that Jesus would have everything under his control.

* * *

One ever-present problem is how to integrate a seafarer into a Bible-believing church. There's the time factor, since the seafarer is away for nine months or more, and then back at home for a few weeks or months. How can a seafarer, who is actually more of a stranger to his home (see chapter 10), become integrated in a church there? And even if there is a church near his home, there's no guarantee that it will become his spiritual home. Then there are the relatives who do not approve of the seaman abandoning his family traditions to attend a faithful church. And should the seaman, who is finally back at home with them, join a church his family don't even know?

And so it sometimes happens that a seafarer, who came to know the Lord through a Bible study on his ship or at some port, later decides to keep his faith to himself and acts as if nothing has changed because he is afraid of the difficulties he may have with his family and relatives. If the seafarer doesn't receive good biblical teaching in his hometown and then hides his new-found faith from his family it will be even harder for him to be open about his belief when he's on the ship again. Then, in a matter of time, he will be overwhelmed by problems and his faith will wither.

4

The Background to Seafaring

Seafaring has existed since the beginning of humankind. Noah, as the first seaman, had command of the ark. In Genesis 6:13-17 we read:

> So God said to Noah, 'I am going to put an end to all people, for the earth is filled with violence because of them. I am surely going to destroy both them and the earth. So make yourself an ark of cypress wood; make rooms in it and coat it with pitch inside and out. This is how you are to build it: The ark is to be 450 feet long. 75 feet wide and 45 feet high. Make a roof for it and finish the ark to within 18 inches of the top. Put a door in the side of the ark and make lower, middle and upper decks. I am going to bring floodwaters on the earth to destroy all life under the heavens, every creature that has the breath of life in it. Everything on earth will perish.

Through the faith of this man, humankind as well as the animal kingdom was rescued. Noah is a prophetic picture of the Redeemer, the Lord Jesus Christ. And the ark Noah built was huge, a novel thing for the people of that time. However, it can be compared to the sailing ships of today.

Psalm 107 gives us an impression of the perils at sea. In the vividly described scenes we are able to understand how the seamen felt, and we can literally hear them crying to God in the midst of danger. Verses 23 to 32 dramatically illustrate how helpless a ship and its crew can be when the wind and waves toss them to and fro. In the book of Jonah we find another very clear description of what seafarers experience when the sea becomes unpredictable. Such situations are not uncommon on the high seas even today.

Throughout the centuries there have always been seafarers. However, in earlier times their work was more acknowledged, since people were more aware of their existence.

Why do men (and women) become seafarers?

It is not so easy to answer this question. Many seamen, especially those from Asia, Africa and South America, go to sea because they want to earn money and improve their standard of living at home. Many fathers want their children to have better opportunities than they had when they were young. Another reason is that many men don't have the possibility to earn decent money at home in their native countries. This draws them away from home without thinking about the consequences for their families. And then, after they have been on a ship for several months, it becomes considerably harder for them to find a job in their home country. For other men being away at sea for 10 months is a means of avoiding domestic and social problems. There, on the ship, they hope to escape from the difficulties at home. Obviously, this won't really solve anything. An additional problem for a seafarer is finding a wife – because what woman would like to be continually separated from her husband? This constant separation makes it difficult to maintain a good relationship. A desire for adventure is something that would motivate very few people from third-world countries to take up a career at sea.

The situation on board the ships and at sea – communication, pay, problems

Many of us on land are not aware of the working conditions of seafarers. And most people from western countries would certainly not be willing to work under the conditions that seafarers have to endure. Several seamen have told me their troubles and complained that they don't feel safe on some of the old and poorly maintained ships. We received the following letter from Anton Dianold from India:

Dear Martin,

Forgive me for answering your letter of October 27, 1998, so late. I received it on December 3rd in Japan along with the Bible correspondence lesson 'Plant My Feet on Higher Ground'. The last two trips were very long. We sailed for 40 days. Then we left Murmansk on February 9th and now we are on our way to China, which we will reach around March 24th. During this trip we stopped in Singapore for a few days to unload and load up again. Murmansk is located in northern Russia, seventy degrees North. It is the northernmost port in the world. On the day we arrived there the temperature was -44 degrees Fahrenheit. I don't have to tell you how cold that is or how all of us from India suffered because we didn't have any warm clothing. I had to stay in the hospital for eight days because the fluid in my knee was frozen. Now I'm OK. I've heard from my family, they're doing fine, and that they are just counting the days till I come home. Yesterday I talked with my daughters on the phone. The younger one said, 'Daddy, you will be home in 41 days.' That made me cry … they miss me so much. I am so glad that this time at least I'll be home for Christmas.

Then there's the fear of going down with the ship. When I was visiting a small tanker, the second engineer, full of worry, told me that the ship was in a miserable condition and he was afraid that he and the whole crew could end up sinking. 'Could you help us?' was his request. I tried to make him understand that my possibilities were limited but I would do what I could. First we prayed that God would take the situation into his hands. Then I contacted the Seafarer's Union to enquire about help. The next day the second engineer greeted me, beaming, and said, 'Do you know what, Martin? When you called the union, it got the captain scared and he bought me an airplane ticket so that I can fly home today.' Shipping companies are afraid to be branded as black sheep if it becomes known that one of their ships is in a bad condition.

The following report appeared in the journal *Hafenarbeit* ('Harbour Work'):[17]

---

[17] 2000, p. 10; *Hafenarbeit* is the German magazine of the International Trade Federation.

There is nothing worse for seafarers than to be stranded thousands of kilometres from home without money, fuel, food or water. The crews on ships belonging to the more disreputable shipping companies have to be prepared for such events with increasing frequency. Every month reports concerning as many as five ships which have been abandoned are registered with the ITF. The fate of seafarers is especially precarious during times of economic downturns or sinking cargo rates,[18] when many shipping companies[19] with ageing ships go bankrupt.

Crews on ships with flags of convenience[20] get the worst deal. During the visit of the *Global Mariner* in Vancouver, the ITF took the opportunity to publicize the situation of several stranded seamen. At that time the first officer of the *Atlantis Two*, Ashley Burgess, came on board and reported that he and his crew had been left waiting on their ship in the Canadian port since November 1997. The shipping company preferred to abandon the crew rather than to pay $450,000 for repairs and wages. During the first seven months of their journey, the *Global Mariner* encountered three abandoned ships. From July 1995 until the end of 1998 the ITF got wind of 199 cases of abandoned crews – a total of 3,500 seamen. The estimated number of unreported cases is no doubt higher, due to the fact that the ITF is not always informed about every case. Panama, where most of the flags of convenience are registered, has the highest number of stranded ships, 70 in total. Some shipping companies even attempt to 'starve' their crews in order to get rid of them so that they don't have to pay them. The ITF urges the international shipping community to establish funds to aid stranded seafarers.

Every year the ITF manages to obtain back payment for crews (to the order of millions of dollars) through their campaign against flags of convenience. In 1998 the total sum of late wages for seafarers came to $42.5 million. This amount may seem enormous, but it included the wages of several thousand seafarers – some of whom had to wait more than a year for the

---

[18] The payment for transporting goods on a ship.

[19] The owners of the ships.

[20] Ships that are registered in countries where the low tax rate is especially advantageous for their owners.

money due to them. For each individual seaman the wages withheld means the difference between a normal income and a life of poverty. During the week-long campaign against flags of convenience at the end of 1999, numerous cases of withheld pay were exposed. For example, a Ukrainian seaman and his two colleagues from the Cape Verde Islands were able to divide $10,900 among each other: they had worked ten months on a general cargo ship that was registered in the so-called German second registry[21] without receiving adequate pay. The ship was detained in Finland. In addition, a Russian ferry with a 59 strong Russian and Estonian crew was held in Sweden until the crew received the $254,879 due to them.

Flags of convenience are especially notorious for paying late; after all, their aim is to sail with the lowest costs possible. The majority of complaints that reach the ITF come from ships flying under the flags of Panama, Cyprus, Malta, Bahamas and St Vincent – the leading flags of convenience. In 1998 a sub-group of the ITF which monitors such ships and their practices dealt with complaints involving a total of 35,000 seafarers. Almost half of these were about withheld pay. Faced with increasing financial misdealing, crews feel obliged to seek help from the government or ITF. In some cases their attempts to obtain fair treatment are supported by personnel at the ports or other employees. In 1999 solidarity campaigns were organized in 29 countries to deal with the problem of withheld wages.

It is not only a scandal that the unions are obliged to act on behalf of the seaman before they can receive their pay but it is also shameful the way many seamen are recruited and hired as cheap labour. From an article out of the ÖTV newspaper *Seefahrt* ('At Sea') we read:[22]

Labour is, so to speak, a cheap product of employment agencies or brokers, better known as modern slave traders. This system is established as an element of international shipping, although it

---

[21] This allows German shipping companies to offer the non-German crews the same rate of pay as their home countries.
[22] *Seefahrt* 2, July 2001, p. 10: ÖTV Report.

Seafarers from the Pacific island of Tuvalu.

is officially prohibited by various conventions. Unfortunately it is common practice for seafarers to pay one or two months' wages or sums of up to $2,000 to a mafia-like employment agency in order to obtain a job. In addition to that, there are the 'passport seafarers' who either do not have maritime training or who have forged papers. Professor Lane from the University of Cardiff estimates that in some countries where seamen come from, up to 80 per cent of the training certificates are either a forgery or the real certificates are sold at a price of approximately $75. A further problem is the 'black lists' that such employment agencies keep, with names of about 10,000 seafarers who are to be denied work.

In October 2000, while I was visiting a ship from a Greek shipping company, I had no idea of the hardships the Filipino seamen would soon encounter. In June 2001, when the ship was back in Hamburg, the men told me about the unbearable situation on board. For most of them the eight-hour working day turned into a twelve-hour day, for seven days a week. But the men might not have protested if they had received decent wages. Instead, they had to go on strike and inform the union. They were forced to demonstrate against unfair wages. The lowest rank, an OS (ordinary seaman), earned $320 per month for twelve hours a day, seven days a week. On top of that, life on board became intolerable due to faulty heating and poor drinking water. The captain denied the union inspector entry to the ship and, consequently, the harbour police had to be called. During this time I had some good opportunities to speak with the crew and to pray with them. Many wanted to have a Bible. It sometimes seems to us that even the almost inhuman living and working conditions lead people to seek Jesus.

It is shocking to read in one ITF magazine,[23] that 15 per cent of all ships are like slave ships. That is the alarming conclusion of a study carried out by an independent commission on the conditions in the worldwide shipping industry. For one year the international commission on shipping matters evaluated the testimonies of witnesses, as well as various reports and documents from governments, companies and unions from all over the world. On the basis of this data they compiled a paper entitled 'Ships, Slaves and Competition', and presented it at an international symposium for shipping safety that took place in March 2000 in Sydney. In the paper it states: 'Ten to fifteen per cent of the seafarers on international fleets are treated like slaves. The safety precautions taken at their workplaces are minimal, they receive little or no pay, they work extremely long hours, they receive very little food, and they are raped or beaten.'

In another ITF magazine[24] we find bits of news that make us sit up and take notice: good news, like 'More Jobs for Women at Sea', and bad news, like 'Rampant Discrimination'. There are increasing numbers of women on cruise ships – yet they are poorly paid. The growing numbers of cruise ships from many different countries is the reason why shipping companies now turn to women to fill the jobs which otherwise would remain vacant. According to a study of 60 cruise liners, 20 per cent of the crew today are women. Women from western countries earn more

---

[23] *Transport International* 5–2, 2001, p. 4.
[24] *Seafarers Bulletin* 14, 2000, p. 19.

Seafarers strike to campaign for better living and working conditions.

than women from other countries, even if they do the same type of work. The scale of pay varies greatly, from $270 up to $2,400 a month for equal work or the same position. This means that waitresses from France, Germany or England earn more than double the amount their counterparts from the Philippines, Thailand or Indonesia earn. Women also work seven days a week. Many have made it clear to the ITF that they by no means intend to work for more than six years on a cruise liner. The reasons given included the hard and demanding work they must do, and their families back home whom they miss too much.

* * *

At the end of the 1980s I read in the press about a particular ship, the *Nicolas P*, which had been anchored in the port of Hamburg for several weeks. The shipping company was insolvent, and Filipino seamen had been asked to guard the ship until it was sold. I managed to visit them by means of a boat, which brought provisions. When I boarded, a seaman carrying a flashlight greeted me. He told me that they had no electricity. As he led me to his cabin he described their situation, which I found unbelievable: during the night the two seamen who were on board had to sleep in their clothes and cover themselves with blankets. In the morning the blankets would be frozen! Those men appreciated my visit very much and later expressed their gratitude in a letter, saying that 'apart from a Catholic priest, you are the only one who took care of us.' After three long years the men were able to leave the ship and return home.

Time and again seafarers report cases of discrimination by their superiors. I once met three Filipinos who told me that they were poorly treated by their captain, a German. This problem upset them so much that they began to pray, asking God for a solution. And after we met for Bible studies a few times, two of the three men asked the Lord Jesus to come into their lives. Time and again God seems to use difficulties to draw people to him. Nevertheless, that doesn't justify the behaviour of those captains or officers.

The pay on the ships is extremely low in comparison to western standards. When you consider that seafarers often work six or seven days a week, you can imagine how frustrating their situation can be. On several occasions I have been called to a ship, only to hear from seamen that they hadn't been paid for several months and they had no idea how they were going to feed their families. The only thing I could do was to call the seamen's union in order to obtain at least a small amount of money for the men and their families.

In one incident, the shipping company was bankrupt and sent most of the seamen home. Three men from Nigeria remained on board to guard the ship from plunderers. But they were at the mercy of the Nigerian authorities, who didn't pay them at all during the last ten months of their time on the ship. In desperation their wives wrote letters, bitterly complaining that they were at their wits' end. One of the men had seven children with his wife back home in Nigeria. His wife didn't believe that he was unable to fly back home; she thought he was living it up in the West. She wrote to him saying that since he wasn't coming home she was going to have to look for another man to feed the family. Another seaman on the same ship reported that he received a letter from

Nigeria telling him that since he wasn't home, the land he had wanted to buy for building was sold to someone else. In this situation we thought the best thing we could do was to offer practical help: we brought them food and clothing, and gave them money – which was an absolute exception.

Every time we have been able to help people like this, opportunities for sharing the gospel have opened up. For example, the crew of a Greek freighter went on strike because of the terrible living and working conditions they had to put up with. One seafarer told me that he earned less than $1 per hour for overtime. Furthermore, the captain forced the crew to work 100 hours overtime a month. When I finally met with the crew, they told me that they hadn't received anything to eat since the morning, so I went out and got food for them. My reaction impacted the men so much that they let me pray for them and read a passage out of the Scriptures. They all listened intently as I read to them. Since most of the seamen were going to be flying home to the Philippines, I gave them a few contact addresses where they would be able to receive practical everyday assistance and hear the gospel as well.

A seafarer from India who came to Hamburg once asked me to get a neck brace for his father. I gladly obtained one for him. A few years later, when his ship was in Hamburg again, he recalled the time I had helped him. It had impressed him so much that this time he accepted Christian literature from me and was open to hearing the gospel. Since that occasion we have become friends, and I have had several good opportunities to tell him about what it's like to live as a follower of Jesus. That little favour I once did for his father has been a vivid example of the message I later preached.

We try to offer very practical assistance, especially to people from other cultures and religions, by helping them with shopping or making telephone calls, or giving advice about certain everyday things, because it fosters an atmosphere of trust.

In some cases the hygienic conditions on board a ship are dreadful. A Filipino seafarer once called me into his cabin and asked me to get in touch with the union. It seemed that the quality of the drinking water was dubious and some of his comrades already had stomach problems. In other cases seafarers have asked me to get them medicine for their various ailments. They were unable to go and see a doctor themselves because they were either too busy working or they didn't have the time because their ship was going to leave soon. Sometimes the captain and officers don't even care when a seafarer has health problems. Assistance then can only be obtained by the intervention of the union.

I have already mentioned that one of the difficulties for seafarers of several nationalities who are living together is that of communication. Furthermore, there are the cultural problems which are often underestimated by western officers. For example, a Filipino male cannot bear to be yelled at by his superior. It can lead to an escalation of the situation and – in one case this really happened – the Filipino seafarer might even try to kill the officer. An electrician from the Philippines told me that one evening a colleague of his who was drunk tried to attack him with a knife. We often hear of cases of seamen who have become violent for one reason or another, either out of frustration, fear or drunkenness. Once a drunken seaman from an island state stabbed another seaman to death. On a motorboat I once heard the captain insult a seaman from the Kiribati Islands. The captain told him: 'You stink.' Even though the seaman had drunk too much, he didn't deserve to be talked to like that.

Prostitution on ships and on land

A very serious problem for seafarers is prostitution and the diseases connected with it, such as AIDS. In foreign ports it is common to find male and female prostitutes who come on board the ships. Seafarers who are away from their families for months on end are especially in danger of succumbing to the temptation, although of course, it can't be said that this happens to all seafarers. However, when a seaman has been together with a prostitute, he is often later plagued with a guilty conscience towards his wife as well as towards God. Seamen have sometimes asked me to pray for them because they didn't otherwise know how to become free from their guilt. Many have shed bitter tears while confessing their sin, and then have asked me for advice on whether they should tell their wives or not.

One seaman, who came to know the Lord Jesus Christ in 1988, told me that in addition to his wife and their child he had a girlfriend and a child with her. Now he asked me what he should do about both women and their children. He felt it was important to take responsibility for the upbringing of both children.

There was another seaman with whom I once shared fellowship and prayer before his ship sailed. The next time this seaman arrived in Hamburg I went to his ship, looking forward to seeing him, hoping to have some time reading the Scriptures with him and praying. My hopes simply vanished when I discovered that he had a prostitute in his cabin. He was so ashamed that he didn't even dare to look me in the face, much less explain anything to me, and we never had a chance to talk again.

My wife, Monika, and I were once visiting a banana ship when we met a seaman from Honduras who said he was a Christian. He invited us to his cabin and we gladly accepted his invitation. When we entered the room, however, we were in for a surprise. Didn't the man tell us that he was a dedicated Christian? On the walls of the cabin there were pornographic posters! That, of course, made us doubt his sincerity. But then Ramon began to explain. When he joined the crew he was serious about his faith, and he intended to be a witness for Jesus Christ. Then his comrades decided to test his faith. In the evening, after work, someone would come and hang a pornographic poster on his door. As soon as Ramon discovered it, he would tear it down and throw it away. But his comrades didn't let up. Ramon would take down the poster in the evening and the next day a new one would be hanging in its place. This went on for so long that he began to see the pictures in his mind. Soon his will was broken, and not only was there a picture on his cabin door, hung there by his comrades, but there was one inside his cabin too. Ramon continued to read the Bible, but he noticed that there was now a kind of barrier between him and God. On that evening, Ramon sincerely repented and took down the pornographic pictures. In their place he hung Christian posters. Later, in our home, we had a wonderful time of fellowship; it was lovely to see how repentance can renew a person. The joy of the Lord returned where there was once an empty heart.

Since that time, Volker and I have met many seamen who, as Christians, have suffered under great temptations in the area of sexuality. We have made it a rule to pray the sinner's prayer only with men who were willing to clean up their cabins as well as their lives.

Of course temptations aren't restricted to the area of sexuality. Alcohol can also be a danger for seafarers. Recently, while aboard a German container ship, a seafarer confided to me that he had a problem with alcohol. He drank every day and wanted to give it up because he was afraid he'd lose his job otherwise. Another serious temptation for seafarers is to be free-spending with their money when they arrive at a port. Some of the seafarers never really had any money at home and, as a result, they don't know how to manage it properly. I have often heard about seafarers who have been forced to extend their employment contracts simply because they had spent all of their money and were too ashamed to return home to their families without anything left for them.

Dangers at sea
The greatest dangers for seafarers are bad weather, poorly maintained ships and accidents caused by human error. Every year there are ships that don't manage to survive the storms. The reasons for this are quite diverse. For instance, if a ship is too old and the containers on it have been improperly loaded, it might not withstand a storm. I have heard many stories about ships being tossed about in the waves like a ball.

In 1995 a ship of the Nigerian National Shipping Lines got into danger in the Bay of Biscay. The engines had broken down and the ship was drifting, unable to manoeuvre in the tossing sea. The electrician on the ship later reported how the whole crew gathered together in one room and in desperation were wildly crying out to God. Muslim as well as Christian seafarers were praying. Some of the Muslim seafarers were even heard promising God that if he saved them, they would surrender their lives to him. And later, three of them did actually surrender their lives to Jesus Christ.

I once received a letter written in Liverpool, from a seaman who used to visit us at home. In the letter he said that he was looking forward to returning home and visiting his family. Unfortunately, this seafarer never made it home. His ship, the *River Guara*, sank in the Bay of Biscay and 20 seamen lost their lives. As happens in such situations, when the breadwinner of the family is no longer there, the dependents, like the wife of this man, are left with no support whatsoever. This woman didn't

know how she was going to feed herself and her son. Certainly
Nigeria has no system of government welfare.

Another African seaman told my wife and me an incredible
story. While a storm was raging, the wind and waves pulled him
into the sea. To his amazement the next wave threw him back on
deck! This miracle made him think seriously about God. He then
surrendered his life to the lordship of Jesus.

Sometimes a fire mysteriously breaks out on board. Once I
was on a Chinese ship, distributing literature in the language of
the seamen. A few weeks later I read in the newspaper that the
ship had sunk. A fire was given as the cause. Perhaps my visit
was the last chance for the seamen to find out about Jesus.

Another ship, the *Acina,* had to be towed from the USA to
Hamburg a few years ago. Fire had broken out in the engine room,
resulting in the deaths of three seafarers from the Philippines.

An increasing danger for seafarers is piracy. Again and again
we hear of attacks and plunder of ships. In spite of tight security
measures, heavily armed pirates still seem to be able to board
and enter ships. In the *Hamburger Abendblatt,*[25] the following was
reported:

> The mere thought of such dangers brings fear and dread: silent
> footsteps, a blow with the machete, gunshots, possible death —
> simply for a watch, cash or a shipment of goods. The pirate strikes
> by surprise and with violence. The number of pirate attacks all
> over the world is on the rise. Willingness to use violence and
> brutality is also increasing. Last year alone the International
> Maritime Bureau registered 469 attempts. In 1999 it was only half
> that. During the first half of 2001 there were 165 assaults registered,
> including kidnappings, in so-called high risk areas. A cargo ship
> is like a supermarket to pirates in the poorer parts of the world.

Nine seafarers die in attacks by pirates
Nine seafarers were murdered in pirate attacks during the first
nine months of last year, according to figures from the
International Maritime Bureau (IMB). This compares with just
one in the same period of 2000.

---

[25] September 5, 2001

The bureau's latest report on armed robbery against ships appears to show an improving position, with incidents falling to 253 in the January-September period of last year, against 294 a year earlier. However, the general level of violence has become much worse, rising from 207 to 294 incidents.

In an attack described in the report, the general cargo vessel, *Atlantic Pride,* was boarded by pirates off Ecuador. The alarm was sounded and the electrician and bosun,[26] followed by the master, started to approach the gang with pressurised fire hoses. Without warning, the pirates opened fire, wounding the electrician and the master. The latter was shot three times in the chest and once in the leg.

In another such case an armed gang seized the tug *Mayang Sari* and the barge it was towing in Indonesian waters off Natuna Island. All of the 10 crew were bound and blindfolded, forced into a boat and held hostage ashore for 10 days. They were later abandoned in a mangrove forest and warned not to tell the authorities what had happened to them or their families would be killed.

Pirates shot and killed six fishermen off the Philippines, leaving their bodies aboard two vessels that were stripped of their engines.

The International Maritime Bureau (IMB) report confirms again that Indonesia and the Malacca Straits are the most dangerous waters in the world, although there is a decrease in the number of attacks thanks to increased patrols by countries such as Malaysia and Singapore. Assaults in the period fell respectively to 71 from 90 the previous year and to 14 from 32.

However, the bureau calls attention to a new trend whereby pirates are demanding ransoms for kidnapped crew members. Particularly risky are waters off the Indonesian province of Aceh, where separatists say ships using the Malacca Straits must seek permission from them in return for safe passage. The IMB reports two hijack and ransom incidents within two months, and suspects that more have gone unreported because owners have been threatened. The risk of such attacks has led the bureau to advise ships not to anchor along the Indonesian coast unless absolutely necessary.

---

[26] The officer in charge of looking after the equipment and general maintenance of the ship.

A seaman wrote the following letter to my co-worker, Volker Lamaack:

I have been a Christian for 15 years. My conversion came about only through the power of God and not by anyone explaining the gospel to me. Before my conversion I had read the Bible, but only for the purpose of debating about it. In June 1985 my wife packed my suitcase because I had to return to sea. I told her to pack some pornographic magazines too. Instead, she offered to pack a Bible. That made me angry and I told her I didn't need a Bible.

While my ship was in Jakarta, I was on duty in the engine room. Pirates entered the ship and asked me where the storeroom was. I answered that I didn't know, since I was new on board. They didn't understand me very well so they continued to ask me all kinds of questions. Every time they asked a question, they hit me in the face or stomach. Finally they tied my hands behind my back, and then my feet to my hands, stuffed a rag into my mouth and pulled me up on a rope so that I was hanging in the air. The leader gave orders to kill me as soon as the engine room was plundered.

My strength was drained and I could only think about dying. Just like a dying man, I began to think about God and scenes from my life began to go through my mind. Then I saw the scene with my wife, as she offered to pack a Bible in my suitcase. God was showing me what kind of man I was – a sinner. I began to cry, not because of the physical pain I was feeling but because I was a sinner, who was going to die soon. I asked for forgiveness for my sins. I began to pray and said, 'I know I have to die but have mercy on my family and me.'

After this short prayer the alarm in the engine room began to sound. It made the pirates panic and they ran around like crazy. Even the man who was supposed to kill me suddenly disappeared. I hung there alone for four and a half hours until my colleagues found me at 5:30 the next morning.

Later, in the hospital, I remembered that I had turned off the alarm for my night shift, so it shouldn't even have rung at all. Yet in my hour of need, God himself made the alarm go off. He did it, not only to rescue me from the pirates but also to save my soul and the souls of my family.

While on strike these seafarers are listening to the word of God.

He did more wonderful things for me during my hospital stay in Jakarta until I was sent home to the Philippines. After this traumatic experience I surrendered my whole life to him and received Jesus as my Lord and Saviour. Since then, the Lord has protected me at various times, for example, during the war between Iran and Iraq when my ship was in that area. Later, when I was flying in a DC10 from Philippine Airlines, there were problems with the engines and smoke entered into the cabin. Both the crew and the passengers began to panic. I began to pray and suddenly I felt an inner peace, and the Lord protected us all. God has worked many wonders in my life since that time. If I were to tell them all, it would turn into a long story. I have learned many things up until today. Whenever I work on a new ship, I start up a new Bible study group. I even do it when there are only a few willing people.

Clichés about seafarers

From time to time I have to deal with the clichés people have about seafarers: they are all rough, hard drinkers, and have a beard. Of course this stereotype isn't correct, even though you might sometimes find men like this. Actually, seafarers are people just like you and me. They long to have someone who will listen to them, they need fellowship and they need someone who understands their problems. Many seamen are married and have children. They don't go to sea because they are looking for adventure but because they have to feed their family and want their children to get a good education. The ships of today, with their modern technology, require seafarers who are well trained and responsible. Therefore, seamen can't be drinkers – at least not while they are working. I am convinced that people need to change the image they have of seafarers and learn about their living and working situation in order to communicate with them.

5

Called to Seamen's Missions

It was at the end of the 1970s, as the unemployment rate was rising, that I finished high school and had to think about further education for a future job. After sending off more than twenty applications to companies, I finally obtained a job at a Hamburg ship brokering company and could begin my training. Being a shipbroker wasn't exactly my dream job but, rather than land on the street with nothing, I took the chance. I did my training from 1977 to 1979 and was surprised to find out that the shipping world could be quite interesting. The company where I worked and did my training was a sort of intermediary between the shipping companies and the clients who wanted to have their goods transported. So it often happened that when a ship arrived at port a colleague would take me along with him to discuss the loading and unloading of goods with the captain. The more I visited those giants of the ocean, the more they impressed me by their sheer size and by the multi-faceted life on board. But never in my wildest dreams did I imagine that someday I would be working full-time on ships like these.

After finishing my training I got a job in the accounting department of my company, as they needed someone who could speak English. I learned a lot there about business and commerce and later on this was very helpful to me. But one day my dreams were shattered when someone came to me and said: 'Mr Otto, we have to forge this cheque.' My conscience was troubled and I knew that as a dedicated Christian I couldn't do such a thing. In the end, someone else forged the cheque. However, my troubles didn't end there; occurrences like that repeated themselves because unethical business practices and fraud against customers were tolerated.

One morning during my devotions I read in Luke 16:10: 'Whoever can be trusted with very little can also be trusted with much, and whoever is dishonest with very little will also be dishonest with much.' This verse made a deep impression on me; God was speaking through it. I knew what I had to do. I immediately resigned from my job since it was impossible for me to be honest there. My employer tried to keep me and offered me a higher salary, but I was sure that God had called me out of that place. In December 1979 I left the company.

Through a pianist, who was also a Christian, I got to know an American family who invited me to stay with them in England from January to June 1980 so that I would be able to improve my English. I accepted the invitation with the hope that afterwards I might be able to get a good job again. There in England I was able to learn very quickly as no one spoke German to me. The family was involved in a little mission that distributed Christian literature, and on Saturday evenings we regularly went to the pubs in order to tell people about Jesus Christ. It gave me good opportunities to try out what I was learning.

One morning during breakfast, an idea occurred to me: 'Why don't I go to the ships in Hamburg with the same literature, just like I go to the pubs here?' The thought of it thrilled me and I found myself constantly trying to figure out how I could put it into practice. When I returned to Hamburg and began a new job in the accounting department of a forwarding agency, my desire was still there. I asked Martin Kohn, a friend of mine, if he wanted to go to the port with me in order to tell seafarers about God's word. Martin spoke good English because he had spent his childhood in Australia. He immediately said yes, and so we made it a habit to go out to the ships for two or three hours on Monday evenings after work.

What we encountered in the port left us speechless. We never thought that we'd be coming into contact with so many nationalities; we were thrilled that the seafarers were so hungry for God's word.

I soon realized that I needed some theological training, since the questions being asked were complex, and so I thought it would be a good thing to attend a Bible school. After working at my job for only 13 months, I left for Switzerland where school began in October 1981. There I learned about missions, disciple-ship, evangelism and different methods of evangelizing. Prayer, discipleship and missions were the main points of emphasis at this school in Walzenhausen. We were taught how important it is to always be prepared to tell others about Jesus Christ and evangelistic activities gave us opportunities to put into practice all that we were learning. The flexibility that we learned at the school would later be very helpful for my work in seamen's missions.

During my second year at Bible school we were sent on a missions trip to Kenya. This eight-week stay would decide the future for many of us, since we were finally able to experience first-hand what missionary life was like. I remember visiting a village where an African put me on the spot and asked me to preach, right there and then. I didn't have anything prepared so I had to pray and ask God to give me wisdom. Then I opened my Bible and simply began to speak. In view of cultural issues this time in Kenya was very valuable for my later work among seafarers.

On Friday evenings missionaries who were working in different parts of the world would come and tell us about their work. After their talk we would then have a prayer meeting. I found these talks fascinating and I always prayed, 'Lord, should I go to China or Africa or Turkey as a missionary?' But whenever I prayed, I felt as if God were replying, 'You know where you should go. Go to Hamburg, to the ships there, to take my word to the seafarers.' This inner certainty actually made me very happy because it made me feel sure that it was really God's plan for me!

* * *

In 1984 I finished my degree. My intention was to return straight to Hamburg in order to begin the work among seafarers. But somehow, for the first time, I suddenly didn't feel at peace about it. I didn't understand anything anymore. I had been preparing for this for three years, and now it seemed God was saying no to my plans. It really shook me. I had always been obedient, I had left everything in order go to the Bible school, and now I was

Crew members relax in the mess room.

unsure. After much thought and prayer I decided to go to Augsburg to join a work of church planting. There I learned a lot about Catholicism. Up to that point my knowledge had been theoretical only, but in Augsburg I learned what it meant to work among Catholics. When I look back today I am very grateful for this 'detour'. Approximately 40 per cent of all seafarers we meet are Catholic. If I hadn't spent time in Augsburg then, I wouldn't have known how to talk with them today.

During my stay in Augsburg I was also sent to India for three months to lead a team of students from the Bible school. This was another valuable opportunity to gain experience in another culture. My faith was sometimes put to the test when I had to eat food that wasn't exactly clean.

In 1987 it finally seemed the right time to move back to Hamburg. I felt inner peace about going and starting my work. In the meantime Martin Kohn and my brother Thomas had done a lot of good preparation work. However, I still had one thing to decide, namely which missionary organization we should work with? The 'we' included my future wife, Monika, whom I'd met in Augsburg. I contacted several missionary societies and spoke with them about my work. The feedback I received was usually very similar: 'We have never heard of the type of work you want to do. I am sorry, but I'm afraid we can't help you.'

So, when my wife and I began our work, all we had was our trust in Jesus Christ, who had given us this calling. We were convinced – and still are to this day – that he would take care of our needs and see to it that this work would be carried out. The year 1987 held a two-fold blessing for us: in May we were married, and in July we were able to begin our work in the seamen's mission. From the very start I was sure of one thing: without a spiritually devoted wife this work would have been very difficult to do.

6

Building Friendships

Seafarers are often away from home for long periods of time, generally from nine to twelve months, and in extreme cases even up to three years. Because of this, many of them long for friendships not only during their time at sea but also beyond that. They are looking for companions in their rough surroundings. And their wives at home also like to know that their husbands have friends abroad. Of course there are also seamen who for the wrong motives are looking for friends. For example, we have received letters from African seafarers, asking for financial assistance or begging for things such as stereo equipment. After all, we are their friends and no one is supposed to let a friend down!

The desire to have a friend is usually genuine, without any ulterior motives. Seamen realize that it's not easy to make it alone in their difficult surroundings. They are suddenly faced with questions they had never considered while at home. How will their family manage without them? How can they make sure that their children will have the right upbringing and not be influenced by someone they don't even know, someone they themselves can't exercise influence over because they are away at sea? Seamen have sometimes asked me, either personally or by letter, for advice on whether they should quit their job even if it would be financially difficult for their family. The idea of being with their children, their wife and relatives, every day, being able to exert a positive influence on the family, is often worth considering.

Questions about the meaning of life and about eternity also begin to occupy the thoughts of many seafarers. Especially Christian seafarers often have a need for friendships because they are lonely, being made fun of for their faith by their comrades and sometimes suffering discrimination. They are encouraged when I show them John 15:15 in the Bible where we see that Jesus would like to be a real friend: 'I no longer call you servants, because a servant does not know his master's business. Instead, I have called you friends, for everything that I learned from my Father I have made known to you.'

This is new for many seamen. Because they view Jesus as God, it makes him seem very far away. Yet the loneliness many seamen experience gives us the chance to show them what happened in our lives when Jesus became our friend. In practical terms, what happened and what changed through our friendship with Jesus? Such questions interest seafarers! It is much more important to show Jesus as a friend simply than to preach about him.

Willy from the Philippines wrote, 'First of all, I'd like to thank you for the Bible you gave me. It is wonderful and I have learned so much by reading the Bible. May God bless you, his instrument. You are a servant of Jesus who teaches his word. Martin, I hope we can be friends because I need a real friend like you. I hope we will see each other again because I would like to be a servant of Jesus. I know he will accept me. I want my life to change. Please Martin, write back. I look forward to hearing from you.'

Another seaman from Norway wrote, 'I received your letter at this port. Thank you, I appreciate it. I sent your letter on to my wife and children and told them about you, my new friend in Hamburg. I would love to visit you and meet your family, but unfortunately because I have so much work to do I can't. I hope that at least we will be able to see each other next time. I am looking forward to it.' This man wrote two long pages, telling me how happy he was to finally have contact with someone who understands him and who also will be able to help him grow in his faith.

Contacts through letters are crucial in keeping up friendships with seamen. Through letters we can greatly encourage them, help them get through lonely times and show them that they are not alone. For a seafarer, one letter means so much, much more than we can imagine. After 40 days at sea, when a seafarer arrives at a port and finds a letter waiting for him, a letter from someone who genuinely cares for him, who understands him and prays for him, it is a wonderful feeling. Seafarers often tell me that they

Sharing the gospel with seafarers during their coffee break.

don't just read our letters once, but over and over again. Then they tell their wives and relatives about the letters. And sometimes they even send our letters to churches back home to show that there are people in the world who are concerned about their spiritual welfare.

In all the years that Volker and I have been working in the seamen's mission we have received thousands of letters. In addition to that, we also get lots of phone calls from seamen telling us they will soon be in Hamburg and they want us to visit them. A friendship is something very special to a seaman, something he really appreciates. We have received calls from all over the world, from Taiwan, the Philippines, Ethiopia and even from European countries. Our friends simply want to let us know they feel close to us. Recently, when our phone rang at 1 o'clock in the morning, the caller, a seaman, didn't have an urgent problem he needed to tell us about but just wanted to tell us he was now on a new ship and was doing well!

It is interesting to notice that when we give some seafarers a Bible they see it as a gesture of friendship, because it shows them that at least someone cares for the welfare of their soul. In many letters and personal contacts on the ships the seafarers often express their gratitude. Here are a few excerpts. Ronald writes: 'Hello, how are you? I hope you are well and I am praying that you remain in good health. I was very glad to receive your letter, and I thank you for answering me. I thank God that you are honest with me. I follow your advice. I would like to be born again and accept Jesus as my Lord and Saviour and follow him. What can I do now? Please, Martin, remember me in your prayers.'

Another seaman, Jack, writes from Taiwan: 'Michael and I were very happy to find friends like you and Monika in Hamburg. I really appreciate your help in sending packages to China and Taiwan. It was also kind of you to show us around Hamburg and invite us to your home. You are the only foreign friends I had during my training there. As soon as I arrive in Taiwan, I will tell my friends and relatives that I have friends in Germany. I am thankful to God that I met you.'

These letters impress upon us the importance of building up friendships with the seafarers. Arnulfo once wrote to us: 'Thank you for your encouraging letters that gave me strength to withstand temptation. I know that my sins are forgiven because I confessed them to Jesus and he has forgiven them. I have the Bible you gave me and have begun reading in it. I am now in 2 Kings. After you wrote to me, advising me to read the New Testament first, I read Matthew, Mark, Luke and John. Now I am reading Acts. I look forward to reading the book of John once more.'

And finally, Anton from India wrote: 'I am so happy to be considered a part of your family. It amazes me, because I met with you and Monika for only a few hours, and that was many years ago. Nevertheless I still have the same feeling as on the day we met. I have met so many people in my life, but I have never had the kind of fellowship with others like I have with you. In addition to that, Jesus has changed my life. Jesus is a part of my life, and he is the centre of my life.'

7

Visiting the Ships

Getting off to a good start is important for whatever project you are involved in. So, one of the questions we ask ourselves is, how do we begin to build up contacts with seafarers? What is our goal? What things do we have to keep in mind so that the open doors for the gospel aren't closed in our faces?

In order to avoid falling into the trap of activism, I think it is crucial to begin the day by seeking God, having fellowship with him and receiving wisdom from him. Therefore, I begin my day with a prayer for God's guidance: 'What ship should I visit, Lord? Which seafarers are open for you and your word?' After my quiet time with God I have always sensed where God wants me to be. Yet it sometimes happens that my original plans change and that I visit different ships. It is also wonderful to experience God's working in the smallest details of daily life. For example, I have often read something in the Scriptures that was just perfect for me, my family or even for a seaman. At times I receive an inner hint to take along a certain thing to read which may be crucial for the seafarers.

After my time with the Lord, the next thing I do is get myself organized for a day on the ships. I check a so-called ship registration list, which is sent to me by fax. This list contains names of all the ships that are currently docked at the port, tells the time of their arrival and their exact location. It helps me to decide which ships to visit, according to where I think God wants me. Of course we also follow certain guidelines in choosing the ships. For example, I first try to find out if there are any Christians I already know on the ships who need encouragement and fellowship. Then I check to see whether there are any seafarers who have had contact with seafarers' missions who now need following up. I also have to bear in mind that there might be a seafarer who has received a

Bible lesson and who might want another one. A final thing to consider is whether there are seamen from countries where they have no opportunity to hear the gospel. These men have priority over those who have such opportunities in their home countries.

The flags which are flying, and the colour or size of the ship help me to recognize which company is using the ship and which nationalities might be on board. However, I don't always find out the exact nationalities of the seamen until I go on board myself. It can happen that the ship has an English name, is sailing under a flag from Cyprus, and has a Russian crew, although I thought it would have a Filipino crew.

In order to do my work effectively it is necessary to have Christian literature and Bibles in the languages of the seafarers. A good start is ensured with a friendly greeting, perhaps even in the language or dialect of the crew.

Sometimes my first contact on the gangway takes me to the recreation room where the seafarers are having their coffee break or lunch. There I greet them and tell them why I am on the ship, although it generally becomes clear when I spread out my literature. I always have in the back of my mind that this ship is their home and, in a sense, I have entered their living room.

Then the men come up to me asking a variety of questions, ranging from 'Can you tell me how to get into town?' to 'Do you have a telephone card for me so that I can call my wife?' or 'Can I have a Bible?' If no one approaches me then I simply ask them if I may briefly share something. Since seafarers are quite friendly they usually agree to my request. Using a rope trick I then begin to explain the gospel, and that gets their attention. Sometimes it even brings tears to their eyes. At the end of my talk, which takes five to ten minutes, I can see who is really interested. Some leave the room, while others, full of curiosity, ask me probing questions. Some want to begin reading the Bible. I offer them a Bible study course and those who are interested in learning more about the word of God give me their names and addresses.

Finally, it is extremely important to find out where the ship will be sailing next. This way I can tell the seamen's missionary in the next port which seafarers were interested in the gospel so that they may be followed up. I also let the missionary know what needs there are on board that he can possibly take care of.

After about 20 minutes the coffee break is over and the seamen return to their work. I leave the ship and go to the next one.

8

Bible Correspondence Courses – Teaching and Following Up

Note: We would like to acknowledge the valuable contribution made by our friends at the Emmaus Bible School, who have provided many of the Bible correspondence lessons we use.

'Teach them to obey everything I have commanded you.' We want to take this command from the gospel of Matthew seriously. If it is important for men and women living on land to obey the good teaching of the Scriptures, how much more vital is it for seafarers who seldom have the opportunity to attend a church? For this reason we have made teaching our priority. It is interesting to note that in the Bible the word 'teach' appears more frequently that the word 'preach'. But how do you teach people you don't even see – people who are far away from home for months at a time, far away from churches or ports where they might be able to receive teaching?

One question we are always asked is how we do follow-up work. How can we keep in touch with seafarers and help those who have just received the Lord or who are very close to making a decision? It's not easy when they have only spent a few hours or a few days at port and then have to go to sea and be there without any Christian fellowship. A few effective aids are radio, television and video. In the Philippines special radio programmes are broadcast for seafarers who are working abroad. Some seafarers have been reached by Christian television in the USA. Without a doubt the Internet will be crucial in doing follow-up work in the future.

Over the past 15 years we have tried out different ideas in order to find the most effective method of following up because, after all, the Bible says that we should make disciples and not just converts. We often used to give a seaman a particular book to read during his trip thinking it would be the right thing to help him. Then we found out that he didn't read it, either because it was too thick and he didn't have the time, or his English wasn't good enough to really understand it.

We also gave certain seafarers cassettes with recorded sermons – and still do today. Although it seemed to be of help, we wondered whether it was enough? What could the seaman do after he read the book or listened to the cassette? How would he grow? We found out that when seamen didn't get anything else they slowly fell back into their old sinful habits because they weren't yet established in their faith. This didn't surprise us – after all, no one could expect any of us to become strong in our faith simply by listening to a cassette or reading a book shortly after being born again. No one feeds a baby one large meal and thinks it's all he or she will need to grow.

So we finally realized that books and cassettes were just a short-term solution. And we understood that what we needed was a long-term training concept which would help the seafarer grow and remain encouraged after four, six or eight months. Through it he would be strengthened, he would be learning, and finally he would begin to tell others about his relationship with Jesus.

In 1988 we began with correspondence Bible studies for seafarers. We found they offer several advantages:

- They enable us to keep in touch with the seafarers.
- The answer sheets help us to see how much of the gospel has been understood.
- The seafarers use these courses and teach others on their ships.
- The seafarers take these courses home and share them with their families and friends.
- These courses help the seafarers to improve their English.
- Through reading and studying the Scriptures seafarers come to a living faith in Jesus Christ.

The last point is very important to us. We sometimes find that the seafarers who have come to a genuine faith in Jesus Christ while doing this correspondence course are more sure of their faith than those who have prayed with a missionary to receive Jesus Christ. The reason is very simple. God's word works changes in people through the Holy Spirit. The danger with seafarers who were led to the faith through another person is that though intellectually they may have understood their need they may not really have sensed it in their heart. In no way, however, do I want to play one method off against the other. God has used both.

As a rule we first offer introductory Bible lessons, which explain the basic truths – why a person is lost and must turn to Jesus in order to be saved. Through these so-called basic lessons many seafarers have received Jesus as their Saviour and they have later told us this in letters or in person when we see them on the ships. After that we give or send the seafarers lessons dealing with subjects such as the church, prayer, Jesus' Second Coming, discipleship, giving their testimony, marriage and the family.

It is always a joy to see what God does in people's hearts through his word. The following example is from Jorge, a Filipino, who added a few lines to the lesson he sent in: 'I started work on

A large containership leaves the port of Hamburg.

this ship on May 20th and when I entered my cabin I found a
Bible lesson which must have been left by the person who stayed
here before. The lesson was entitled "The Bridge". I began to read
it, and became more and more interested. I decided to study it
and answer the questions, but unfortunately, I didn't have a Bible
with me so I couldn't look up the verses. Could you please send
me a Bible? I want to continue this course as I have never read or
studied the Bible until now. I hope you will understand. May
God bless you.'

Every year Volker and I receive hundreds of these correspondence lessons to correct. Dozens of seafarers have received
Jesus Christ as their Lord and Saviour and have served as
witnesses to their relatives, families and friends.

Avelino, also from the Philippines, wrote: 'I miss my family
very much, but I miss my Bible course even more. Could you
send me a new lesson immediately?'

A ship with people from the island state of Tuvalu sailed from
Hamburg to Marseilles in France, where I contacted the local
seamen's missionary because I didn't have any Bibles in the
language of the crewmen. I asked him to visit those seafarers.
The following answer was written on a postcard from Marseilles:
'The ship has arrived in Marseille and nine seamen asked me for
Bibles. They all spend their free time doing the Bible lessons.'

On another ship someone sent me a short note: 'Please send a
Bible correspondence course to my friend who is with me on the
ship.' These courses aren't just for non-Christians; we also send
them to Christians so that they will be strengthened in their faith
and motivated to give testimony on their ships.

Allan, a young man from the Philippines, told us: 'I am looking
forward to the next lesson. I have to tell you that the last lesson
was a great blessing because it revived my faith. My life has really
changed.' We see that changes really do take place in the lives of
the seamen when we meet them again on the ships. It is
encouraging to experience the power of God's word.

On a German tanker I met Andy, who later sent me the following
letter: 'Dear Martin, how are you? I hope you're well. Do you know,
I have been so blessed by the seamen's mission. It is really
wonderful to come closer to Jesus. I have been working at sea for
12 years and no one has ever given me a Bible correspondence

course until now. And since doing the lesson, my prayer time has been transformed.'

In another letter a man from the Philippines wrote: 'Thank you for the Bible. Now, little by little, I can get to know God's word better. I was lost for so many years, but I think that it is never too late to come to Jesus. I hope very much that you will send me a new lesson.'

From India we received this news: 'Since I have begun to study the Bible correspondence course, I have noticed that my life has changed. My faith in Jesus grows every day because in each lesson I read many Bible verses. I am grateful to God that I got to know you, since you gave me the chance to encounter Jesus through the Bible studies.'

Another man from India, whom I've known for a long time and who once asked how he could become more familiar with the Bible, recently wrote me a letter saying, 'I give you the right to call me "son" because you have given me spiritual food. I have shared important things from the Bible course with my friends in my prayer group. They are also interested in receiving Bible courses even though they aren't seafarers. Is that possible? Or can I just photocopy my lessons and send them to my friends? I want them to be blessed just like I have been through these lessons.'

A lesson may not always be understood immediately, which is evidenced by the following comment from an Indian seaman: 'I tried to understand the book *Messianic Psalms* but it was difficult. After re-reading it several times I finally understood the point. This course is not only informative but it has promoted my spiritual growth. I used to think that the seamen's missionaries just wasted their time when they tried to help seafarers who weren't interested in changing anyway. But now I know I was wrong. When only one seaman in a hundred is converted, it is a great success. Heaven rejoices over that. You can count me as that "one" now.'

Here is another reaction: 'Martin, I can't find the right words or even express myself the way I'd like to. The only thing I can say is that I am feeling good and that there have been many changes in my life since I have begun to study the Bible course. Even my comrades have noticed changes. They say I used to be quick-tempered but now I've become gentle.'

A seaman from Tuvalu accepted the first lesson from me, filled in the answer sheet and sent it in. He wasn't really interested. I encouraged him to do lesson two and he only completed it as a favour for me, he later told me. However, during the third lesson the Holy Spirit clearly spoke to his heart and convicted him of his sin. At that point we received the following lines from Keith: 'I really want to be saved from God's judgement, because I have been a sinner from my birth. Yes, I am a sinner, even today. Lord, save me!' The seamen's missionary from Sydney, Australia reported to us that Keith told him how he received saving faith and how Jesus transformed his life. Keith has now completed his 16th lesson, and he says he is so excited about it. He studies the Bible systematically and learns vital things about God, about himself, about the church, missions, the Second Coming of Christ, and many other things. Recently Keith wrote to Rob Flinders, our seaman's missionary from Australia, and asked him to have me send his wife the same lessons, in the same order, because she wants to study the Bible intensively too.

A seaman from the Pacific Ocean state of Kiribati wrote us the following: 'I would like to thank God and praise him with my whole heart and my soul. The last lesson – "How to Grow in Faith" – helped me to open my whole heart to Jesus. I have been lost. Please pray for me and my family at home.'

Time after time we find that seafarers who aren't really that open to God's word accept Bible courses anyway. Then they start studying them and suddenly begin to hunger for more of God. This comes out in talks and letters from seamen. Ianea Iotua from Tuvalu wrote: 'Please send me all of the Bible lessons. Just as I have sent in this answer sheet, I want to study all of the lessons. Please send me the lessons even when I am no longer on the ship but back at home, because I would like to learn more about God and Jesus. I will wait for your answer to find out whether you will fulfil my request or not. I would also like to learn more English so that I can understand the Bible better. I hope that this correspondence course also enables me to improve my English.'

I met a seaman on a Nigerian ship who fully immersed himself in the Bible studies. He completed one lesson after another. When he was back in Hamburg and I asked him to give me his answer sheet so that I could correct it, he refused. I asked him why. He told me that through the course his life had changed so radically that he was afraid that if he gave me the answer sheet to correct he might not get it back. He held the paper, pressed to his chest, and I began to understand what God's word can do in a person's life.

One thing that gives me great joy is that seamen often take these courses home with them to their churches and share the blessing they have received with others.

We know seafarers who have not only become Christians through these courses but have also received training in the faith and become mature believers and adults. The result is that they become evangelists on their ships, at home, in their neighbourhood and among their friends. Many seamen have become so motivated through these courses that they have given up their work as seafarers to go into full-time service spreading the gospel of Jesus Christ.

* * *

It is especially important to encourage seafarers to do the Bible correspondence courses simply because they are seldom in one place for a long time, which would otherwise enable them to attend a church and receive instruction in the Scriptures there. Many seafarers would like to be able to visit a church. For this reason I encourage them to start Bible study groups on their ships. Some of the seafarers are afraid to and tell me that they don't feel strong enough in the faith – they think they need to know more before they can begin to teach others. I just give them a Bible correspondence course and tell them that now they can systematically learn about the Bible.

I received this report from a Filipino: 'Things have changed here on the ship since you encouraged us to begin a Bible study group. Every Sunday we meet to study the Bible. The first engineer leads it. At the moment there are four of us participating. By the way, could you send us the lesson "One God, One Way", which you already sent me. The second officer wanted to have it and he sent it to his family. I would like to study it more carefully because there were a few things in it which really interest me.'

Pat, also from the Philippines, wrote in his letter, 'I have received the lesson but I am not yet finished with it because things have been hectic here on the ship. One thing I do notice is that the more I study the lessons, the more I understand what it means to be a Christian. During all these years I don't think I ever really knew God, even though since my childhood I thought I was a Christian. But since I have been working through these lessons and reading the Bible that you gave me, I now understand more about God's love for me. You asked me in your letter how I can become a child of God. I think by confessing my sins to Jesus and receiving his salvation.'

We received the following comments from a seaman on a container ship:

Greetings in the name of Jesus,

I am your student (Mr Obaaria) and would like to thank you and say that I find your Bible course very interesting. I can't tell yet whether my life has changed, but I do notice that I am living in the light more and more. I am waiting for the correction of my lesson and then I will try to understand the corrections. I also need some more lessons.

Thank you! Sincerely, Tiaoniti Obaaira

Sometimes we don't hear anything for a while after giving someone a lesson to study. This happened with an engineer from the Philippines. In 1993, when he was working on a passenger ship, I gave him a lesson to work on. After seven years I received the following letter: 'I still have the Bible correspondence course you gave me. I wanted to answer it and send it in but never got around to it. But, do you know, I have taught 20 people with this lesson and would like to receive more material. These 20 people hunger for more good teaching from God's word.'

9

The Work Grows

One of the most astounding experiences I've had with the Internet is that one can hardly find any information about evangelical seamen's missions there. For a while I searched in vain using various Christian search engines from the USA, England, South Africa, Canada, Australia and New Zealand. Whenever I typed in the word 'seafarer' I received only a few hits.

Despite the fact that almost every day we share the gospel with unreached people on ships at port here in Hamburg, this type of missionary work remains relatively unknown. If one considers how easy it is to spread the gospel to the unreached who are located in the various ports, it is hard to understand why worldwide there are so few seamen's missions.

Shortly after beginning our ministry here we already realized that we would need co-workers if we wanted to work effectively. Often we didn't know which ships we should visit because there were so many anchored here. I remember how one seaman wrote and scolded me: 'Why didn't you come to my ship to have fellowship with me? I was alone in Hamburg and was looking forward to your visit.'

At other times we were extremely busy and could only painfully acknowledge the fact that opportunities to teach the Scriptures were neglected due to lack of help. Actually, back in 1987 when we began, we immediately started praying for co-workers. We were encouraged by Jesus' words in Matthew 9:38: 'Ask the Lord of the harvest, therefore, to send out workers into his harvest field.' There has always been a large harvest in Hamburg

Then one day in the autumn of 1990 – at a birthday party – we met Volker Lamaack, who would later become our co-worker. The following is his story.

* * *

Ever since my youth missions had fascinated me. I especially enjoyed reading the biographies of missionaries like Hudson Taylor. I just devoured those books. At the time of that party, I was 30 years old and married. My wife also shared my interest in missions. Would God ever call me into the mission field? We were open to it but had never felt the call. After being trained as an organ builder and geriatric nurse, I didn't want to take any radical steps unless I received a clear calling from God. Besides that, didn't a missionary first have to get a degree at a Bible school or a seminary? And even if God called me, I'd still have a number of years to go in terms of studying, training, applying to missionary organizations and waiting.

We had already known Monika and Martin Otto for some time. They visited the church where my wife and I had been members for a long time and gave a slide show to tell about their work among seafarers. We found it exciting to hear how open the seamen were for the gospel. After that we began to support them financially, but as anonymous supporters. Yet I never thought that this type of mission would be the thing for me; it was just so different from anything I'd ever known. Although I had spent almost all of my life in the port city of Hamburg, I had never even talked to a seafarer. Right after I finished school I did a two-year period of practical training in a shipyard, but ship building is not the same as sailing on a ship.

Around that time Doris and I met with two to four other Christians several mornings a week to pray for about 45 minutes a time. In the autumn of 1990, after one of these meetings, a friend and I had breakfast together while the others went to work. Suddenly, out of the blue he asked me, 'Why don't you go and visit the ships with Martin Otto? Would that interest you?' Strangely enough, the idea did seem interesting. Later that morning I called my wife at work and told her about it. She told me that during our prayer time that morning she had had the same idea.

A few days later the Ottos, my wife, and I were invited to that birthday party where I took the opportunity to talk to Martin. His reaction was interesting: 'The port in Hamburg is very large and I just can't manage all the work myself. We've been praying for co-workers for some time now and have had you in mind.' He'd never told me that before.

An empty bulk carrier passes under the Köhlbrands Bridge.

Things began to get exciting. However, I wanted to be careful not to rush into a new activity and then later have to back out because it wasn't for me. So we decided that I should try to re-arrange my schedule at the hospital where I was working, in order to have more free time. I would do the night shift four times a month for half a year. That way I could visit the ships with Martin and at the same time be praying for further guidance. My employer agreed to it, although I later found out that they soon expected me to return to my normal schedule.

Before I talked with my supervisors at the hospital, my wife and I had discussed our idea with our parents and with the elders at our church, both of whom had supported our decision wholeheartedly.

On the 2nd of January 1991, about three months after the prayer meeting I have already mentioned, I was leaving the house to go to the ships with Martin for the first time. Doris told me she had just read a verse she wanted to share with me. I don't remember exactly which verse it was, but it said something like this: Go to your work with confidence, because God is with you.

That morning, on the second ship we visited, Martin had a
talk with the second officer from Ghana. They were talking about
believing in God. God gave us grace and I had the privilege of
being right there when this man gave his life to Christ. I couldn't
think of a more encouraging start to this work.

The following weeks and months gave me a lot to think about.
My English was poor, so I began to brush up on it. I didn't know
much about the seamen's countries, cultures or religions. And I
knew even less about their lives, their work and their
surroundings. Here are some of the questions I had:

*How do you find your way around the port? (It is almost 48 square
    miles.)*
*How are you supposed to get from place to place at a container terminal?
    (There are a lot of things to watch out for.)*
*Where do you park your car when it's always in the way, no matter
    where it's parked?*
Which flags tell you the nationality of the ship?
How can you tell by the flags which nationalities will be on the ships?
How do you greet and speak to the seafarers according to their ranks?
How do you even start up a conversation with a seafarer?
*How can you understand English-speaking seafarers with their different
    accents?*
*Who speaks which language? You don't just know that in the Indian
    state of Kerela most people speak Malayalam.*
How can I organize my material, which is in 50 different languages?
*How can I understand the reaction of a seaman to the gospel? Is his
    friendliness simply culturally conditioned or is he really impacted
    by the message?*
Which verses are helpful in explaining the basic truths of the Bible?
How do I deal with difficult theological questions?
*How can I help a person who is a Christian but under the influence of
    unbiblical church traditions?*
How can I raise support in case I want to go into the work full-time?

So many questions remained open as Martin left for a week to
attend a conference on seamen's missions in Canada. That meant
I had to go to the ships alone, for the first time.

On that first morning I had a very intensive time of prayer as
I presented the following request to God: 'Lord, if you want to

use me among seamen, then please give me grace so that I can lead a person to faith in you.' God worked a miracle and a seaman from the Philippines was converted. From that moment on my doubts were gone. The Lord confirmed the work of my hands in many ways. Like a puzzle the pieces fitted together.

In October 1991 I handed in my resignation at the hospital. After that several things seemed to point to the fact that I was going in the right direction: my mother told me something which she'd never mentioned before, how right after I was born she dedicated me to the Lord, just as Hannah had done with her son Samuel in 1 Samuel 1. After thirty years the Lord fulfilled his purpose for me in this way. I also began to see how God had given me natural abilities and spiritual gifts that are useful in the field of seamen's missions.

During the following years God expelled any doubts Doris and I ever had about my going into this work. Up to this day we have enjoyed this ministry and have experienced so many encouraging things. God is gracious to us!

10

Hospitality — The Key to Winning Hearts

In order to reach seafarers effectively with the gospel, we always
have to ask ourselves whether the seafarer – no matter which
country he comes from – understands the message we are trying
to get across. Culture plays a very important role in this matter.
If we are not in a position to understand the seafarer as an
individual who has been formed, among other things, by his
culture, then how are we going to bring the gospel closer to him?

A vital element of every culture is hospitality. When Volker
and I are on the ships, we immediately notice how hospitality is
a way of life to the seamen; it doesn't matter whether they are at
home, in a foreign country or on the ships. For this reason we
have made it our practice to show hospitality by inviting them to
our homes whenever they have the time. The seamen appreciate
it very much, and I think this is one of the reasons why they
open up to the gospel. Even in the Bible, hospitality is
emphasized. In Romans 12:13 we read, 'Share with God's people
who are in need. Practice hospitality.' And in Hebrews 13:2: 'Do
not forget to entertain strangers, for by so doing some people
have entertained angels without knowing it.'

The wife of an Indian seaman once wrote us a two-page letter
expressing her appreciation for our having had her husband as
our guest. In 15 years at sea he had never been invited to someone's
home. We had wonderful fellowship with him and when he had
to go back to the ship we were able to give him a Bible in English.
He was so impressed by his time with us, even though it had been
short, that he began to write to us. We corresponded regularly and
after about five years he asked, 'How can I get to know the Bible
better?' At his request I sent him a lesson from our Bible correspondence course, which he promptly worked through and sent

back for correction. I sent him additional lessons and after working through several he wrote back, telling me that now, after so many years, he finally understood that he wasn't a Christian. It resulted in a clear decision to surrender his life to Jesus Christ, which bore fruit that even his comrades noticed. After more lessons he wrote, 'You feed me with one treasure after another.' And then he wrote, asking us to pray for him because he was considering becoming a seaman's missionary in India.

I met Noodle on a Taiwanese bulk carrier. He had this nickname because supposedly his father owned a noodle factory. Noodle wanted to learn English and so he asked me if I would speak English with him to help him improve. Of course I agreed, and we talked about a lot of different things. That evening I invited him to our house and we had a good time together. Over dinner we talked about his home, Taiwan, as well as many other things. We even read the Bible together – he read in Chinese and we read in English, and then we compared what was written. It was a lovely evening and we all enjoyed it. Around midnight I took him back to his ship and he thanked me for our hospitality.

After about two months I received a letter from Noodle in which he asked, 'Why did Monika cook such a good meal for me and why does Martin love Jesus? Please answer my questions because it is very important.' A few months later, when Noodle was able to return home on leave, he wrote us another letter. 'Martin and Monika, I have shown two Korean missionaries around my country and invited them to my house. They asked me why I did it, since I don't even know them. I answered them: I did it because my friends in Hamburg, Martin and Monika, did the same for me.' We were speechless at how important hospitality can be to a person. Since then we have kept in touch with Noodle, especially through letters, and we hope and pray that the love of God, which was shown through hospitality, will help this seaman to find Jesus.

On a Greek ship I met Mario Albay, a Filipino Christian, who told me about his problems on the ship. While we were talking in his cabin he told me that he had been made fun of, mocked and even physically threatened. Someone once even tried to take his food away from him simply because he was a Christian. So, Monika and I decided to invite him to our home. There we read the Bible together, and we tried to answer his questions as best as we could. We also prayed together. When he left to return to his ship he was strengthened in the faith and joyful. Finally, after so many months, he was able to have fellowship with other Christians. After that he wrote many letters and expressed his gratitude for the fellowship and hospitality because it had really encouraged him in his faith.

In October 1987 we had a rather exciting time with people on a ship from Ghana. We invited the first officer, who was there with his wife and children, to a service led by Bruno Herm, who was the head of the German Missionary Society at that time. After several days of fellowship with this man and his family, the ship sailed and we received a letter from the wife: 'We arrived in Belgium at 2 o'clock in the morning. My husband is exhausted because he had to work the whole night through. It was very hard for us to leave Hamburg. I couldn't stop crying. When I went into our cabin I saw my husband and our daughter crying too. Rhonda was crying because she had to leave Auntie Monika

A passenger ship with hundreds of seafarers on board.

and my husband and I had to console her. It was a very special time for us and we will never forget you. We will remember you in our prayers. Dear Martin and Monika, may God richly bless you for the love and fellowship you shared with us.'

Two seafarers who were often at our house were Gaston and Edward from Cameroon. They came over so often that they were practically a part of the family. One day when we took Gaston along with us to visit my parents-in-law in Hessen it caused a sensation. A real African visiting a little village in Hessen! It gave especially the older people a lot to talk about. We did many things together with Gaston and Edward, and that drew us close together.

At his home church in Cameroon, Gaston told his friends about his trips in and around Hamburg with us. As a result, they began to pray regularly for the seamen's missions in Hamburg as well as for seamen's missions worldwide. That church is very mission minded and they have a day of prayer once a month for world evangelization. Unfortunately there are now hardly any shipping companies from West Africa that come to Hamburg, since many are bankrupt, and we seldom now have visitors from Africa at our home.

A seafarer from South Africa who had just come off the ship recently told me how happy he was to finally be standing on firm ground again. We love to have seamen over to our house because then we as a family have the opportunity to show them the love of God. At the beginning of our work we often had African seafarers over to visit, which was especially interesting for our children. They were so thrilled that their excitement created a good atmosphere, much faster than we as adults could have done it. When my daughters were younger and an African would hold them in his arms, it made us all laugh. Jennifer and Samira weren't inhibited or afraid and they always wanted to know why the men from Africa didn't have straight hair and looked so different. That made the seamen laugh and then the ice was broken. Sometimes the children asked the guests to play games with them and that was always funny.

* * *

At this point I'd like to take the opportunity to express my thanks to my daughters for their understanding towards seafarers and this missionary work. Thank you, Jennifer and Samira, for always being flexible and willing to give up a family night when I would suddenly call, asking whether I could bring seafarers home with me. You've even had to accept a change of plans at the weekends if I was suddenly called to a ship or when I had to pick up a seaman to take him to church and afterwards back home with us. Thank you too because you didn't just put up with all that but you showed understanding, and you were always friendly to our guests. I don't take that for granted. On the contrary, your attitude has often made my work easier. You are great children; I am proud of you!

I am proud of my wife as well. She is always willing to put up with interruptions during her day, willing to prepare meals for our guests when I suddenly call and tell her that I will soon be coming home with a few seafarers. It is great to know that I can bring guests home with me at any time.

11

The Place of Seamen's Missions in World Mission

The ministry of a seamen's missionary is to meet the social and spiritual needs of seafarers. It is no different from that of missionaries in Africa, Asia and other parts of the world. We want to spread the good news of Jesus Christ as he commanded in Matthew 28:19-20, Mark 16:15 and Acts 1:8. To win people for Jesus and make them into disciples is our first priority, and that takes precedence over all the other things there are to do in the varied work among seafarers. Naturally we cannot and do not want to overlook their social needs. Here it is important to help where we can because, after all, such help has often served to make the message of the gospel clear and trustworthy.

Is it possible through seamen's missions to reach the unreached and to carry out world missions? I can answer an unequivocal yes, because people from all over the world come to our ports.

When we began visiting ships in 1987, we were amazed, not only by the number of ships which anchored there daily but also by the many, many nationalities represented. I hung a map of the world in my office and stuck a coloured pin in each country from which I had met people on the ships. After just a short time I had already met people from 80 countries, and I didn't have any pins left. But I kept meeting people from other countries, even from places that didn't have ports of their own. Many seamen come from places located in the so-called 10/40 window.[27] I also for the first time met people who came from countries I had never learned about in geography at school like the Pacific

---

[27] The geographical area between the 10th and 40th degrees latitude, where many unreached countries are located.

Ocean states of Kiribati, Tuvalu, Samoa and Tonga. It became very real to me that God's word would go out from Hamburg and reach the furthest corners of the globe.

In Isaiah 66:19 we read, 'I will set a sign among them, and I will send some of those who survive to the nations – to Tarshish, to the Libyans, and Lydians (famous as archers), to Tubal and Greece, and to the distant lands that have not heard of my fame or seen my glory among the nations.' Here God tells us clearly how much he wants the Good News to be heard even on the smallest islands.

Paul says in Romans 15:20 that it is his ambition to preach the gospel where Christ is not known. And exactly that is our ambition in Hamburg too! Seafarers, who have never heard about Jesus in their own countries, are able to hear the news that he died for their sins here for the first time.

Many seamen who have received Bibles from me say that it is the first Bible they have ever held in their hands. Just yesterday, while I was visiting a ship with an Asian crew, I met a Muslim seafarer who came from a country where the Bible is forbidden. He said, 'This is the first time that I can read what you have given to me.' When I gave a young seaman from North Africa a Bible in Arabic he told me 'I've been wanting to have one for a long time.'

Through seafarers, we see that the gospel is taken to previously unreached ethnic groups, it is carried to the far corners of the world, and it reaches places we would probably never go to ourselves. Furthermore, the literature that the seamen receive is also passed on in their home countries, and in this way God's word is spread further abroad.

Another North African also asked me for a Bible in Arabic. When I asked him if it was permitted reading, he said no. 'But,' he added, 'simply because it is forbidden in my country, I am interested in reading it.' This wasn't an isolated case. The Bible is particularly interesting to seafarers, especially those from the Middle East or Asia who hardly get a chance to read or buy one. Through seamen I was able to get Bibles into Burma (Myanmar), where it is still sometimes copied by hand. Once, when a ship arrived from there, the officer on duty gave me a bucket full of honey and said, 'This is a thank you from our pastor for the Bibles.'

There is certainly no better way to take the gospel abroad than by ship. The seamen from closed countries spend months at sea and have time to read the Bible, books or other literature we give them, without having to worry about being observed by any state or religious police. Often those very men take the literature home and pass it on to relatives, friends and acquaintances, even though that poses a risk for them. One seaman from a Muslim country recently told us that he was immediately arrested after his last journey because he came home with a Bible. In addition to his prison sentence he had to pay a fine.

The spread of the gospel among seafarers has far-reaching effects. For instance, a seaman from Cameroon asked me for fifty Bibles in French for his church, because no one there could afford to buy one. When he took the Bibles home there was much joy. A few months ago I received a letter from this seaman who reported that this same church made it their goal for 2001 to send out 10 couples to be missionaries.

Besides the literature that we offer, the *Jesus* film is a good way to draw people's attention to the gospel. It seems to work well with Muslims, Hindus and Buddhists, because even if they aren't interested in our message they can still find out something about the life of Jesus. Recently a Filipino seaman came to me and said that a Catholic priest he knew really liked the film and wanted to borrow it for his church. We have even heard that as a result of this film seafarers have prayed in repentance and surrendered their lives to Jesus. Is there anything better to say about a film? We have been able to get this film into many third-world countries through seafarers. It has also been handed out in other ports, so that it has literally been taken to the ends of the earth. Once again, seafarers from all the different countries and islands are being reached with the gospel on their ships while at port.

Seamen not only take the word of Jesus Christ to the remote areas of their own countries but they also do missionary work in other ports by giving witness to the love of God. Again and again seafarers ask me for tracts and Bibles because they want to hand them out in the countries to which their ships are travelling.

It is interesting to note that we meet a multitude of other people besides seafarers on board the ships who also hear the word of God from us. For example, there are the vendors who want to sell things to the seamen. And there are the representatives of the shipping companies and the owners of the ships. Occasionally politicians or important business people visit the ships. A few years ago the Burmese ambassador visited a ship from Burma to see his countrymen. I happened to be on the ship at the same time and someone told me about this important visitor. The Burmese seamen were excited because the ambassador was there. I asked a seaman if I could speak to the ambassador, but my request was refused. So I told the seamen that I had an important gift for the ambassador that only I could present to him. I was finally allowed an audience with him and we sat together and talked. When I presented him with a large Bible in Burmese, he was greatly pleased.

A few years ago a huge, luxurious yacht was built in Hamburg for an oil sheik from a Muslim country. The whole thing was supposed to be a secret. When the ship was finished and ready to leave Hamburg, I decided to go aboard with literature to distribute. Before reaching the ship, I was stopped and told that I wasn't allowed on board – that no one was allowed to see it. Then I decided to pray that God would open a door for me and made one more attempt to get on board. I asked if I could lay out some Christian literature in the recreation room. To my amazement the officer on duty gave me permission. Later I found out that he was a born-again Christian. After this encounter I was able to visit the yacht every day and share the gospel with the seafarers there.

Finally, Volker and I were able to hold Bible studies in a container nearby, and two seamen received Jesus Christ as their Saviour. On one particular day there was great excitement because the owner of the ship, who was also a friend and advisor of the king of his country, was coming to visit. This man flew into Hamburg by private jet and stayed for a few days to visit his ship. I asked if I could speak to him, but that was impossible. Then I tried to find out how I could get a Bible to him. A Filipino woman who was in charge of cleaning his cabin said she would give it to him. A couple of days later I asked the woman if he received the Bible. She said yes, and added 'He not only accepted it but he put it next to his bed, which gives me hope that he might look at it in the evening before he goes to sleep.'

* * *

One great advantage of this neglected type of missionary work is that missionaries can serve in their home country. This makes the preparation time shorter and easier than for other types of missionary service. German, American, Dutch or English nationals can reach people from the third world without even needing a visa. They can take the word of God to seafarers in the ports of their own country. This type of work may be especially appealing for people who would like to undertake missionary work but cannot go abroad for particular reasons, such as health matters. The seamen's missions offer the opportunity to reach people from all over the world within one's own country.

Another advantage is that the local church can be more effectively involved in missionary work and thus make a contribution to world missions. Sometimes we have taken groups from local churches to the ships so that they could hold services for the seamen there. More often, however, individuals who have an interest in missions come along with us to visit the ships so that they can see the work first-hand. When church members see and experience this work themselves, they are more likely to be motivated to support missions either through prayer, gifts or in practical ways. We know families who have invited seamen to their homes. By finding out something about the needs and cares of those seafarers, the families have become more interested in missions.

Churches as well as individual Christians often desire to support missions. The problem is that they don't always have a clear picture of the ministry they are supporting. Here in our work among seamen, people often tell us how happy they are to help because they have seen what we do on the ships and sometimes have even participated themselves. In this way they know exactly how they can support us through prayer, gifts or by practical help.

Some Christians feel they are too old and wonder how in the world they can contribute practically towards missions. Here in Germany we have quite a few very dedicated older ladies who knit hats for seamen and thus do a very valuable service for the Lord. Seamen from third-world countries aren't used to the cold when they come to Hamburg in the winter. A Muslim seaman from Pakistan asked me, 'Why do you love me so much?' I didn't understand his question at first, until he explained what he meant by love – a warm woollen hat, for example. It goes to show that small things done in love can have a great impact on people!

12

A Worldwide Ministry

The missionary organization Seamen's Christian Friend Society (SCFS) in England plays a crucial role in worldwide follow-up work and networking. This organization was founded in 1846 by Charles Smith with the aim of organizing prayer meetings with seamen on ships. Another aim was to keep in contact with seamen by letter. In the aftermath of two world wars, the SCFS was active in only five ports. Fortunately the work has again expanded and 12 ports were actively involved in missionary work in 1990. Today the number has increased to 35, located in the following countries: Great Britain, Ireland, Germany, Belgium, the Netherlands, USA, Australia, the Philippines, Ghana, New Zealand and St Lucia.

The motto of the SCFS is 'World Mission on your Doorstep'. This organization aims to take the gospel to seafarers from all parts of the globe and provide them with fellowship, so that in as many places as possible they may find a warm Christian welcome.

* * *

We believe that spiritual fellowship in a group of believers on the high seas is also a kind of church. This temporary church on a ship enjoys the authority of God and is charged with carrying out his work just like churches on land. As we understand it, this church fulfils the criteria mentioned in Acts 2:42-47:

> They devoted themselves to the apostles' teaching and to the fellowship, to the breaking of bread and to prayer. Everyone was filled with awe, and many wonders and miraculous signs were done by the apostles. All the believers had everything in common. Selling their possessions and goods, they gave to anyone as he had need.

Every day they continued to meet together with glad and sincere
hearts, praising God and enjoying the favour of all the people. And
the Lord added to their number daily those who were being saved.

In July 2001 I visited the *Royal Princess* and experienced a church
consisting of 30 believers from different countries. They would
meet together three times a week for prayer, Bible studies and
Sunday service. On that ship it wasn't only the men but also the
women who were active. The believers there practice a living
faith, making them a living witness for Jesus. It is interesting to
note that they also have a leadership of elders. Similar churches
are found on numerous other ships too. It is encouraging to see
that each group does its part to fulfil the Great Commission and
evangelize among different nationalities by inviting people to
enter into a relationship with Jesus and become his disciples.

Who works in which port?

If a seamen's missionary wants to keep in contact with seafarers, it
is crucial for him or her to know who is working in which port. We
need to know who is stationed in the nearest port so that we can
ask missionaries there to carry on the follow-up work where we
have left off. Thanks be to God that in the last few years workers
in many parts of the world have been called into this ministry.

In January 2001 Rudy Kuijer began as a full-time missionary
among seafarers in Rotterdam, Europe's largest port. In spite of
that, more missionaries are needed. Also in 2001, Rob Flinders
began full-time work in Sydney, Australia, while Ian Dennis is
now working in Melbourne. So we can say that there is a strong
basis in Australia. In Brazil, Luis Santos has been working in
Vitoria full-time since 2000. The prospects for more workers in
other ports in that country are promising. Chris MacCloud and
his partner have begun evangelizing among seafarers in the third
largest container port in the world, the combined ports of Long
Beach and Los Angeles. I could name many other workers who
do a valuable service among seafarers. They work part-time, and
some of them are preparing for a full-time ministry.

However, in the largest container ports of Hong Kong, Singapore
and Kaoshiung, workers are urgently needed. In China and Japan

they are needed as well. In the Philippines we enjoy close collaboration with co-workers. Since 20 per cent of all seafarers are Filipinos, it is extremely important to have a few good bases there in order to do follow-up work. We should by no means forget to keep praying and asking God to send workers into his harvest field among seafarers.

Worldwide networking among seamen's missionaries

Since 1991, when the first international conference for evangelical seamen's missions took place in Canada,[28] the work has grown and cooperation among seamen's missionaries has been strengthened worldwide. Modern communication technologies such as e-mail and the Internet have made great contributions too. Furthermore, the cost of telephoning in third-world countries has decreased tremendously, enabling missionaries to call each other and keep the lines of communication open. There have been international conferences in the Philippines (1995), South Africa (1997) and the USA (2000).

It is crucial for us to understand seafarers in their situation and do our best to be both friends and family to them. They have been completely uprooted. Consequently, we place a high priority on individualized follow-up work through seamen's missionaries in other parts of the world. When seafarers feel accepted and understood it is easier for them to trust missionaries and they are more willing to listen to the message of the gospel. For this reason it is imperative that the missionary watches out for the seaman, in order to assure him that he has not been forgotten. The missionary should try to keep in touch with him, however possible. This follow-up begins with a letter written to the seamen while he is at sea. It continues with a tip, telling him where he can have fellowship in his next port. We have to take the initiative and contact the missionary in that next port, telling him which

---

[28] The term 'seamen's mission' used in this book refers only to evangelical seamen's missionary groups. There are many other seamen's missionary organizations throughout the world and they do valuable work which is greatly appreciated by seafarers. However, the focus of their work is not sharing the gospel.

A passenger ship with crew from many countries, including Indonesia, the Philippines and Cuba.

ship with which crew will be arriving, in order to ensure an effective follow-up. And finally, we try to build bridges to the home church and family of that seaman.

In the Philippines there are seamen's missions located in five ports, working harmoniously together. This ensures optimal conditions for the Filipino seamen. When a Filipino seaman flies home we contact our colleagues there and then they do whatever they can to take care of his spiritual as well as social needs.

It is also wonderful to be able to help integrate families. Our seamen's missionaries consider it vital that the wives, children and relatives also hear God's word and are assisted in every way possible. For this reason they make it a point to visit the families regularly – and the result is sometimes that whole families come to know Jesus: both the seamen aboard ship and their families back home!

Due to so many unknowns in the lives of seafarers, including the uncertainty as to which the next port will be, seamen's missionaries have developed a unified follow-up system. The purpose of this system is to contact and send information to a number of missionaries in different places, so that the chance of finding someone who can then get in touch with the seafarer when he arrives at port is greater.

The system (used by many but not all of the missionaries) works something like this: each missionary sends all the necessary information about the seafarers he has recently met to a central office (presently located in Hamburg). There this information is organized and put on lists which are sent out. These lists contain names of seafarers who are open to the gospel and names of Christian seafarers who would like to have fellowship. In this way missionaries are able to see where seafarers have heard the gospel.

At our last conference, which took place in the USA, an international umbrella organization, Harbour International Ministries, was founded with the intention of being a voice for seamen's missionaries. This organization aims to foster understanding among missionaries for the benefit of the seafarers, while recognizing and respecting the national identity of each missionary. An e-mail prayer-newsletter was also started.

13

Seafarers' Expectations

In 1999 I carried out a survey that lasted twelve months. During that time I gathered information from approximately five hundred seafarers who all came from different countries and cultures. One of the questions I asked was: What do you expect when a seamen's missionary visits you at the port? It was important for me to find out directly from those men and women concerned what their needs and wishes were. This would prevent us from having to speculate about these and run the risk of being way off target.

It was interesting to note that Christians as well as non-Christians indicated spiritual care and support as being their foremost need. Many answered spontaneously: 'I would be very happy if someone invited me to church.' Some answered that they would welcome it if the missionary prayed with them. Others pointed out that the Bible was important to them. 'It would do a lot of good if you read the Bible together with seafarers and used it to encourage them.' Christians answered that they would like to see Bible studies being offered on the ships. And again others asked, 'Could you go to the captain and ask permission to start up a Bible study group on board?' A Catholic engineer wrote the following: 'We expect spiritual motivation that would help us to draw closer to God. Through spiritual support given by missionaries the chances of our being able to flee from sin would be greater.'

Deepak Dayal, an Indian chief officer, wrote me an e-mail recently which gave me something to think about:

> To be honest, I have to say that it is unfortunate that only a few missionaries visit ships today. The number of ships has certainly increased, but there are hardly any missionaries who visit us. Perhaps someone will come and sell us telephone cards. Then, if

you call a missionary, he will come and drive you to the city or to the mission's headquarters. But in many so-called seamen's missions I haven't met a single missionary. What happens is that seamen go to the seamen's mission's headquarters to have a drink and make a telephone call. I remember in the 1970s, when a seamen's missionary would come and visit you on the ships and he would pray with you. He would even give you evangelistic material if you requested it. And on Sundays he would pick us up and take us to church. Nowadays everything is so fast and hectic. We hardly ever stay at a port for more than 24 hours. And most of the time we don't even go on land. We look at our e-mails, make phone calls and relax. At such times it would really be great it someone came on board and talked to us. Seafarers need hope, support and fellowship while at port. They are all lonely. Every seafarer has problems and struggles in some way or another, and it would do them good if they could talk about their problems with a missionary who understands.

Some seamen say they would like to do sightseeing and they expect us to be able to give them directions or drive them to the city for shopping. Seafarers have always been positively impacted when they see that we are willing to give them our time and help them in practical ways.

Others responded that they want to be able to talk with us about their problems on the ships, especially when they don't get paid or when life on board becomes unbearable for one reason or another.

In winter we are always asked for warm clothing. Many Asian and African seafarers leave their homes without any idea how cold it can get in other countries. A few years ago we found out through his wife about an African officer who didn't even have any socks to wear, and it was winter!

While one passenger ship was docked in Hamburg for the winter the heating was turned off for repair work. The seafarers, wearing only T-shirts, gathered in the recreation room. When I arrived with woollen hats, the men snatched them up in no time. I handed out 250 hats on this ship alone. Another day I came with clothing – pullovers, jackets and trousers, among other things. This practical gesture opened the seamen's hearts for the gospel. As a result, I was able to sell 60 *Jesus* films and distribute a lot of literature. Best of all, however, was the start of a Bible study group consisting of participants from the Philippines, Cuba and Indonesia.

14

My Dream

Because seafarers are truly a forgotten people, the aim of my prayers and efforts is to establish a place where they can go in every port in the world. Seafarers should be given the opportunity to have fellowship, hear the gospel and receive practical assistance. This is the only way to counteract common temptations such as alcohol abuse and prostitution. Practically speaking it is almost impossible to achieve these goals because there are many ports in the world where there are no seamen's missions, and there are still countries where freedom of religion is restricted. Yet God is able to reach those seamen whom we officially are not able to reach. For example, one seaman told me that while he was in a Muslim country he heard the gospel from a foreign ship's engineer. This engineer worked on various ships and always carried Christian literature with him, which he passed on whenever he had the opportunity.

At present the focus of our efforts is to send seamen's missionaries to ports where freedom of religion is guaranteed. In order to achieve this goal, churches, Bible schools and missionary organizations need to hear about the wide range of possibilities available to international seamen's missions. We pray that churches located in the various port cities will dedicate themselves to reaching the seamen who are right on their doorstep. We have often witnessed the personal, spiritual and cultural enrichment a church experiences when members become involved by taking seafarers to Bible studies, small group meetings or Sunday church services. It's an eye-opening experience for people to hear a seaman tell about his life. Both parties profit from this contact and fellowship. Individual Christians and families can invite a seafarer to their homes, offer hospitality and share the love of God. The seafarers will never forget this hospitality and will always regard it as a high point in their seamen's service. We still receive letters from seafarers asking about people who had once invited them to their homes.

The relationship between the seafarer and the church is only one side of the coin. The other side is equally important – the relationship between the church and the missionary. How wonderful it would be if churches sent out missionaries – out into the world and out to ports, where the gospel has not been taken yet. How wonderful it would be if students at Bible schools should consider a ministry among these 'forgotten people'. There is a great potential here – the future lies open.

The past clearly shows that missionaries have often had difficulties raising support. Without prayer, financial help and other means of support it is not possible to carry out missions effectively. Sometimes this has prevented people being sent out to the mission field. Such problems have to be addressed – both sides need to be willing to contribute.

Building up an effective means of networking and collaboration among the worldwide evangelical seamen's missions is perhaps a more pressing issue for us in the field. We need to be careful and avoid putting our own plans and ideas first by asking ourselves how we can make sure that each individual seaman gets the fellowship he needs in his next port. Many have made the mistake of simply giving the seaman the name and telephone number of missionaries, without thinking that the seaman might not have the time or even the courage to give the missionary a call. Or he might not have the money he needs in the right currency. It is vital that we, as seamen's missionaries take the initiative by asking the seaman where his next port will be and personally contacting the responsible person there. In this way we can make sure the seaman will be visited and receive the help he needs in case of problems.

From seafarers to missionaries

Our highest goal is to lead seafarers to a living faith in Jesus Christ, making them into disciples and effective witnesses wherever they may be, at sea or at home. No one can reach seafarers more effectively than seafarers themselves.

Gifts of good clothing always bring great delight.

On an African ship I once met a young trainee officer who gave a clear witness of the gospel of Jesus Christ to his whole crew. When I first boarded the ship and asked if there were any Christians on board, a Muslim seaman answered, 'Go to the trainee officer. He is a real Christian.' This man wasn't known simply as being a Christian – he lived his faith in a very active way. Once, when he didn't have a boiler suit for work in the engine room, he prayed for one. And what happened? He received 12 second-hand suits from a man who was doing business on the ship. But what really impressed this seaman's fellow Africans was that he didn't try to sell those boiler suits but instead he gave them away and kept one for himself. If anyone had questions about things concerning the Bible or faith, they went to this trainee officer.

Another 'missionary' I met on a German ship was a first officer from the Philippines. He was a trustworthy, hard worker, and as a result was promoted several times by the shipping company that employed him. Once a week, after his work in the evenings, he invited the rest of the crew to a Bible study, which he led. I was astonished to find out that 90 per cent of the crew attended these studies. I have seldom heard of such high attendance at Bible studies on ships. Even the German officers were so impressed by his faith that they attended the Christmas services he held.

The role of seamen's missions in discipling

First of all, Christians who work on ships need a great deal of encouragement, help and support from us, since it is easy to get discouraged when they are alone. It is important to make it clear to them that God has put them on the ship, given them a task to carry out, and that they themselves can be missionaries. Many are not aware of this. Inviting them to our homes or churches for fellowship, listening to their problems and praying about these concerns are also very helpful.

Secondly, I always try to find out whether the Christian has a good relationship with the church in his home country. In this way he can share his prayer requests with them so that they can support him in prayer and strengthen him. Unfortunately, however, this is the exception rather than the rule, due to problems on both sides. Either the church has little interest in seafarers or the seaman fails to build a relationship with the church. When churches do their part in corresponding with the seamen and providing them with good spiritual nourishment, we see growth. Then the seafarer experiences a living faith that he can share with others.

Thirdly, it is important to teach good doctrine to the Christians on board so that they will be able to grow in faith, be strengthened and then pass on what they have learned. Since the beginning of our ministry, through our Bible correspondence courses, we have helped seafarers in this way because we want them to become mature Christians who joyfully share their faith.

Fourthly, it is vital to convey a sense of vision. The seafarers need to understand that they themselves can begin Bible studies on their ships and can even start up small churches. It is important for them to share with others what they have learned. It is equally important for them to be supported and helped by others on the ship when they are going through tough periods.

Where this happens one normally finds people on the ships whose faith is growing. And then, if we involve the churches in their home countries and they also teach the word of God, the result will be good missionaries on the ships who are witnesses of Jesus Christ in word and deed.

In short, this is my vision for the seamen's missions:

- To have a seamen's missionary or a church in every port in the world, which would see to the needs of seafarers, share the gospel with them, and make them into disciples.
- To establish collaboration among the evangelical seamen's missionaries around the world. Working together, one missionary would pick up where the other at the last port left off, thus enabling the seafarer to have fellowship in every port.
- To encourage seafarers, helping them in spiritual as well as practical matters. To establish home churches that will disciple the seafarers, so that they can be missionaries on their ships and back home.
- To encourage seafarers to start up churches on board their ships.

15

Possibilities for Partnership

Interested readers may now have questions such as:

- What are some things that I can possibly do?
- What can we do as a church in order to carry out the Great Commission among seamen?
- How can churches help and serve seamen's missionaries?
- Are there any projects we can support in prayer and do publicity and/or recruiting for?

First of all, it needs to be clear that a missionary is not a lone fighter. He or she can only carry out missionary work effectively, for example among seafarers, when doing it together with a church. Ever since the beginning of our ministry we have been very fortunate because several churches and especially our home church, the Free Evangelical Church of Haiger-Steinbach, have given us valuable moral and practical support. This support has been a constant source of motivation and it is one reason why we've always had so much joy in our work. It means a lot to us to know that our brothers and sisters in churches at home and abroad share the load.

To carry out this work effectively and to reach the 1.2 million seafarers and their families throughout the world with the gospel, it is imperative that from now on we, as the body of Christ, undertake this work as a joint effort.

Older brothers and sisters in the Lord sometimes ask, 'What can I do to further the kingdom of God?' I believe they can do a lot. Many older ladies knit woollen hats – signs of God's love which open the hearts of the men on the ships. Many, especially older brothers and sisters, strengthen us daily through faithful prayer. Without their prayers many things would not have

What a mission field - 1000 seafarers on one ship alone!

happened; many things would not have been imaginable during the past fifteen years. We need these prayers; indeed we depend on them and hope that many more 'prayer warriors' will be won for this work.

* * *

Since many Christians can't quite imagine exactly what we do among seafarers, we offer to give talks about our ministry within the Seamen's Christian Friend Society.[29] Missionary events at churches, Bible schools and missions conferences give us good opportunities to present our work and share information with others, so that they can pray. Of course, we also consider it important to inform people and raise their awareness about an area of missionary activity that they themselves may even be able to do some day. These events serve to win co-workers, either for prayer, practical assistance or for starting up a new work at a

[29] Information is also available from our website at http://www.scfs.org

port. No concrete help can take place without the necessary information. Therefore we welcome all questions.

We also like to invite people to spend a day with us at the port. This enables our guests to find out first hand what we do. And it adds impact to the impressions and experiences that they, in turn, will share with others. Our guests become eye-witness reporters, and then, when support of whatever kind is provided, it is effective because it is based on conviction.

In addition to the information evenings we hold in churches, we feel it is important to inform Bible schools and missionary organizations about our work. People should know that with modest means and preparation it is possible to carry out world missions effectively. Very often students at Bible schools ask themselves where their paths will take them. Being informed aids the decision-making process.

My wife Monika wanted to go to Africa as a missionary when she was young. Then she found out through me that in the world-class city of Hamburg there are endless possibilities of sharing the gospel with Africans. To the glory of God, Monika and I bear witness to the fact that increasing numbers of seafarers, an oft-neglected people, have Jesus in their hearts and rejoice to do the will of God. Can anything be more beautiful?

In Revelation 5:9-10 we read:

> And they sang a new song:
> You [Jesus] are worthy to take the scroll and to open its seals,
> because you were slain,
> and with your blood you purchased men for God
> from every tribe and language and people and nation.
> You have made them to be a kingdom
> and priests to serve our God,
> and they will reign on the earth.

Appendix

The 20 Largest Container Ports in the World

	1999	2000	2001
Hong Kong (China)	16,210,792	18,098,000	17,826,000
Singapore	15,944,793	17,086,900	15,520,000
Pusan (Korea)	6,439,589	7,540,387	7,906,807
Kaoshiung (Taiwan)	6,985,361	7,425,832	7,540,525
Shanghai (China)	4,216,000	5,613,000	6,334,000
Rotterdam (Netherlands)	6,343,020	6,274,556	6,095,502
Los Angeles (USA)	3,828,852	4,879,429	5,183,520
Hamburg (Germany)	3,738,307	4,248,247	4,688,669
Long Beach (USA)	4,408,480	4,600,787	4,462,958
Antwerp (Belgium)	3,614,246	4,082,334	4,218,176
Port Kelang (Malaysia)	2,550,419	3,206,753	3,760,000
Dubai (United Arab Emirates)	2,844,634	3,058,866	3,501,820
New York/New Jersey (USA)	2,828,878	3,050,036	3,316,275
Bremen/Bremerhaven (Germany)	2,201,120	2,751,793	2,915,169
Jakarta (Indonesia)	2,273,303	2,476,152	2,773,000
Tokyo (Japan)	2,695,593	2,898,724	2,770,000
Yantian (China)	1,588,099	2,139,680	2,744,616

Seafarers!

Felixtowe (England)	2,696,659	2,793,217	2,650,000
Qingdao (China)	1,540,000	2,120,000	2,638,500
Gioia Tauro (Italy)	2,253,401	2,652,701	2,488,332

(Container traffic in millions)[30]

---

[30] Taken from the Hamburg harbour website <http://www.hafen-hamburg.de/html-engl/home.htm>. Go to 'Data and Facts' and select 'Containerthroughput of the world's major ports'.